Sklansky Talks Blackjack

By
David Sklansky

A product of Two Plus Two Publishing

FIRST EDITION

FIRST PRINTING
JANUARY 1999

Errata

1. On page 60 the second line under "Basic Strategy" should say:
   Soft 18: Hit against nine, ten, or ace. ...

2. On page 68 lines 10 and 11 should say:
   ... hit 16 against a ten if there are more fives left in the deck than sixes," ...

3. On page 76 the picture of the A♥5♦ should be the A♥3♦.

4. On page 76 lines 19, 20, and 21 should say:
   ... Basic strategy for two sevens is to split them when the dealer shows a deuce, trey, four, five, six, or seven. ...

5. On page 77 the third line under "Basic Strategy" should say:
   Pair of sevens: Split against deuce through seven.

Sklansky Talks Blackjack
COPYRIGHT © 1999, DAVID SKLANSKY
and TWO PLUS TWO PUBLISHING

For information contact: **Two Plus Two Publishing**
226 Garfield Dr.
Henderson NV 89014
(702) 896-1326

ISBN: 1-880685-21-3

To Joey, wherever you may be.

Table of Contents

About David Sklansky

David Sklansky is generally considered the number one authority on gambling in the world today. Besides his nine books on the subject, David also has produced two videos and numerous writings for various gaming publications. His occasional poker seminars always receive an enthusiastic reception including those given at the Taj Mahal in Atlantic City and the World Series of Poker in Las Vegas.

More recently David has been doing consulting work for casinos, Internet gaming sites, and gaming device companies. He has recently invented a new game called *Poker Challenge,* soon to appear in casinos.

David attributes his standing in the gambling community to three things:

1. The fact that he presents his ideas as simply as possible (sometimes with Mason Malmuth) even though these ideas frequently involve concepts that are deep, subtle, and not to be found elsewhere.
2. The fact that the things he says and writes can be counted on to be accurate.
3. The fact that to this day a large portion of his income is still derived from gambling (usually poker but occasionally blackjack, sports betting, horses, video games, casino promotions, or casino tournaments).

Thus, those who depend on David's advice know that he still depends on it himself.

Other Books by David Sklansky

Hold 'em Poker
The Theory of Poker
Getting The Best of It

Sklansky on Poker
Poker, Gaming, and Life

Gambling for a Living by David Sklansky and Mason Malmuth
Hold 'em Poker For Advanced Players by David Sklansky and
Mason Malmuth
Seven-Card Stud for Advanced Players by David Sklansky,
Mason Malmuth, and Ray Zee

Introduction

There are about fifty people who play blackjack better than I do. There are also about fifty people who know more about blackjack than I do. There are even a few people who both play better and know more about the game. Some of them, such as Stanford Wong and Arnold Snyder, have already written excellent books on the subject. In spite of that, I thought that it was a good idea that you hear from me also. There are three reasons:

1. I believe I can teach better than anyone else, even though there are a few people who are a tiny bit more expert on the game than I. Those that know me know that one of my better attributes is the ability to make complex subjects as easy as possible. Some of the other blackjack books have tried to do this, but none have really succeeded. Apparently no other authors were willing to risk criticism from their colleagues by simplifying, and thus making their advice slightly inaccurate. I don't have that problem. What you will be reading here will be a tad less than perfect. However, if you follow the advice in this book you will win at least 90 percent as much as if you played much more difficult systems put forth by others. In reality you will probably do even better than that, since you are less apt to make errors.

2. Not only do I believe I can explain blackjack simpler, I also believe I can explain it in a more interesting way than what has been previously done. I am not talking about throwing in chapters about my exploits. Rather I am talking about the actual strategy part of the game. First of all, I have dispensed with charts. The fact is that many people find it very difficult to learn blackjack strategy via the method of charts. Even for those who can do it, it is a tedious and boring exercise. I believe it is much simpler and more entertaining to use conversation to explain the various correct plays for all of the

various situations you encounter at a blackjack table. Thus the title, *"Sklansky Talks Blackjack."*

What I have done is to separate the game into all of the possible totals, (i.e. 21 down through 2), that you can be dealt in a blackjack game, and I have written a chapter about each of those totals. Each one will first explain the so-called basic strategy that should be used for that particular total. I will then go on to show when and why that basic strategy may sometimes be deviated from, depending on the "count." Finally, I will occasionally talk about other interesting concepts involving those particular totals. I have little doubt that this technique will make it much easier to learn and memorize expert strategy.

3.   There are a lot of people who have read my work who trust only me, not other authors. This is very gratifying. In the case of blackjack however, they could in fact have done well following other experts (most notably Thorp, Wong, Snyder, Malmuth, Griffin, and Epstein). Still the fact remains that there are many of you out there who wouldn't be convinced about a game until you read a book that I wrote about it. So that is what I am doing.[1]

---

[1]From the publisher: This is also the way that we at Two Plus Two Publishing felt, and so we encouraged David to write this text.

A Note on Notation

Many times in this book I will be using card pictures to represent hand totals. For instance, the text might show the

when I am referring to a total of 9. I do this because I believe that visualizing hands instead of just reading numbers is a better way to learn and understand blackjack strategy.

However, you must realize that in blackjack, since suits have no meaning, any six or trey could have been used. Furthermore, since all totals play approximately the same, no matter which cards are used, the advice given will apply to any appropriate group of cards that make up that total. For example, if I tell you to double down on the 6♣3♦ in a certain situation, it would also apply to the

4 A Note on Notation

or the

and so on.

Part One

Blackjack Theory

Blackjack Theory

Introduction

Before telling you the right way to play blackjack — a way that will actually give you an edge over the casino — I want to tell you where that strategy came from. I want you to get an idea why it works. You don't need to know all this stuff if you don't want to. You can just follow the advice in the next section and spend the money it makes you. But I personally believe it is better to understand where that advice comes from.

Can You Get the
Edge Over the Casino?

There is absolutely no doubt that blackjack is a beatable game. There is absolutely no doubt that you can have an edge over the casino. In other words, you can play in such a way that the percentages are with you. There is no house edge. Rather there is an Emily edge (if your name is Emily). I hope I have made this point very clear. So why, you may be saying, isn't everyone doing it? There are three reasons. One, is that it is not easy. Two, is that your edge is relatively small. Three, is that the casino will stop you from playing if they think you figure to beat them. Let's look at each of these three problems:

1.   To actually get an edge over the casino in blackjack you must learn to count cards. Even if you don't count cards, you can still play very close to a dead-even game if you follow what is known as "basic strategy." This is the strategy that computers have calculated for any particular player's hand against any particular dealer's upcard. For example, if you have

and the dealer has an

showing, the basic strategy play is to hit, not stand.

However, even basic strategy is not all that easy to learn quickly. Memorizing all the various situations that may occur could take quite a few hours. Furthermore, if you go on to become a "counter" you need to get the basic strategy down so "cold" that it will take you even longer.

If you actually want an *edge*, you need to learn how to count, which will take another forty or so hours of practice and experience. In addition, you will need about forty more hours memorizing deviations from the basic strategy based on the count. So we are talking about possibly a hundred hours of complex studying and practice before you are good enough to have an edge over the casino.

Many people are simply too lazy to go through this. I personally find that astonishing, especially as regards those people who play blackjack quite a lot. Even if they have no aspirations of being a professional gambler, if they are going to play anyway, why not play with an edge? That hundred hours of work will add up to tens of thousands, if not hundreds of thousands of dollars, in comparison to what they would have made without the work.

Of course, this propensity of gamblers to be lazy or to be skeptical of mathematics is something you should be grateful for. If many amateurs decided to play blackjack expertly, the casinos would have no choice but to change the rules to keep the game in their favor. Luckily for you, most people are dumb, lazy, or both. And hopefully, I can make some of those hours a little less tedious than they would be if you tried to learn blackjack from another author.

2. Even if you play practically perfect blackjack, your edge over the house is at best 1 percent of your total action.[2] This means that if you were betting $100 a hand, you will earn about $1 per hand. That translates to about $100 an hour. That's pretty good, if you can afford it and get away with it. However, neither is guaranteed. To bet $100 a hand requires about a $20,000 bankroll, if you want to be relatively sure of not going broke. Quite a bit more is needed if your edge falls below 1 percent or if you attack the six deck shoes.[3]

   Furthermore, any bet over about $50 starts to get a lot of scrutiny from the pit. So if you conservatively assume that your edge is three-quarters of a percent, and that you are betting an average of let's say $30, you would need at least a $10,000 bankroll to try and make only a bit more than $20 an hour. All of a sudden the idea of playing blackjack for a living seems less attractive. So not surprisingly there are not that many players who make it a full-time job. However, it certainly is a profitable venture if you can afford the swings (both financially and psychologically), and can find a way to bet more than $50 without getting any heat on you. This brings us to number three.

3. Casinos are aware that blackjack is theoretically beatable. Because of that they will take counter-measures if they think that they are up against an expert player. This is of course

---

[2]Some reputable authors have claimed 1½ percent, but that was years ago. In today's modern blackjack environment, the best players only have at best a 1 percent edge. If you follow the advice in this text, you too can achieve that.

[3]Many casinos will only accept big action in their shoe games. Thus if you want to win $100 per hour this is where you will frequently need to be and to assure safety you will need more than $30,000.

more true if that expert is betting significant money. However, most casinos are not very adept at telling the difference between an expert and a merely good player. Also, big money to one casino means something different than it does to another.

In any case there are ways of operating as a blackjack player that are much less apt to bring serious scrutiny and counter-measures on you, and will extend your welcome in a particular casino, or a particular town, or a particular country for that matter. (Those counter measures, by the way, can range from shuffling more often to actually making you leave the casino.) In general these methods relate to occasional deceptive strategy plays, different techniques as far as how long to stay in a casino, and the use of what is called "team play." (Team play is when a group of expert blackjack players agree to "pool" their bankroll and split-up their wins and losses appropriately.)

In spite of these problems, blackjack is definitely a game you can beat. Certainly if you are going to play anyway, it is inexcusable not to learn how to play properly. Whether you should strive to play for a living is another story. But there is no question you can, at the very least, add to your income via this game. Now let's read on and learn how to do it.

Basic Strategy

The words "basic strategy" mean a lot more to the expert blackjack player than they imply. To the average person those words convey a simple strategy for a game without most of the more advanced complexities. But that is not what blackjack players mean when they talk about basic strategy. When we are talking about blackjack, basic strategy means something quite specific and something not all that simple. It means *the proper strategy for any players' total against any dealers' upcard*. And it is not a matter of opinion.

The only time experts deviate from the proper basic strategy is when they are counting cards and find themselves in a position where it is right to do so.[4] However, this situation does not come up very often. The vast majority of the time expert players are playing their hands according to the basic strategy. In fact, it has been shown that a counter who uses his count only to change his bets, but not to change his strategy, will win at almost as fast a rate as one who sometimes deviates from basic strategy. (The exception is against a deeply dealt single deck.)

It is important to understand that merely playing basic strategy is the main reason you will do a lot better than players who are trying to play by using common sense. Basic strategy was calculated by computer and verified many times over. Again, it is not a matter of opinion. It is true that the proper basic strategy varies slightly, depending on the exact house rules and the number

---

[4]The only other time would be when a professional player is trying to disguise his expertise, and makes a play against what basic strategy recommends in order to throw off someone who may be scrutinizing him. For example, basic strategy says to hit a soft eighteen against a ten. Some pros will disobey this rule, (knowing that it costs them little in the long run), because hitting in this spot is not something that the typical amateur does.

of decks you are up against. This accounts for slight discrepancies you may see if you happen to pick up a few different books by different blackjack experts. The discrepancies are not related to any disagreement among experts as far as what the proper basic strategy is.

In the next section I will show you in more detail the underlying reasons behind basic strategy plays. It would be helpful if you knew them, but it is not absolutely necessary. What is necessary is that you *completely memorize* the proper basic strategy for blackjack before you do anything else. You must practice it as well. It must become totally second nature before you go on to learning how to count and learning how to use that count. Playing perfect basic strategy gives the house only a tiny edge over you. So learn it well, since only then can you graduate to being a winning player.

How Are These Strategies Derived?

You don't have to read this chapter right now if you don't want to. You can become a great blackjack player by simply following the advice in this book, without knowing where that advice came from. However, I believe it is easier to learn blackjack, or most other things for that matter, if you have some idea of the underlying theory. So even if you choose to skip this chapter for the time being, you might want to come back to it after you have read through the rest of the book.

The first thing you must understand is that correct blackjack strategy is *not a matter of opinion*. It is based totally on the mathematical theory of probability. There is no psychology involved. There are no hunches involved. Unlike poker, where experts can disagree on the right play, in blackjack there is only one right play. (Sometimes on very close decisions you will make a different play than another expert because you are using a different counting technique. This is a rare event that will occur even though both of you are following the directives of the particular count that each of you are using. The fact is, one of you is making the "wrong" play by a tiny margin, but that is because no count reflects the remaining cards perfectly accurately. But this is a fine point that has no bearing on the general idea that correct blackjack plays are mathematical and not debatable. Of course, there might be times where you would deviate from the proper mathematical play to throw off casino personnel who are monitoring your action. But in that case you are purposely making the strategically incorrect play for other long run gains.)

Proper blackjack play can only be derived with computers. There are simply too many combinations to work out with a pencil and paper. But it is no big deal for computers. Basically, two different techniques have been used. One involves actual probability calculations. The other involves simulations. Properly done calculations give you perfect answers. Simulations do not.

When I say simulations, in essence I am saying that the computer "deals out" a very large number of hands, plays them in all possible ways, and then records the results. Thus, the results are subject to "luck," just as you would be had you played those hands that many times. However, it is a well known fact of statistics that the more hands you play, the closer your sample results will be to the true probabilities. Now that computers can deal out literally billions of hands in its "mind," we can be quite confident that the results are very very close to perfect. And because simulation is easier than calculation, that is how most blackjack results have been derived.

Another reason we can totally trust the results of these simulations is that quite a few different, highly qualified people have done this work, and they have all arrived at the same conclusions. While I am not one of those who actually did the original computer work, I can tell you that it is inconceivable that the results you will be reading here are not truly the right way to play blackjack.

Let us examine in a little more detail exactly what the computer does when it determines the right play. It does not simply see whether a particular play makes money or wins more often than it loses. Rather, it evaluates a play *in comparison to its alternative*. Sometimes this is very straightforward.

For instance, when the player has a

against the dealer's

showing, he is in trouble no matter what he does. When he hits, he will win about 27 percent of the non pushes.[5] However, when the computer also calculates how often he will win if he stands, it finds that to be about 24 percent of the time. That is why the computer says to hit that 16.

Actually the computer evaluates each situation using what is called *"expected value"* (also called *"mathematical expectation" or simply "expectation")*. This is necessary because of the possibility of pushes (ties), and is even more necessary when we get into doubling down and splitting decisions. Expected value means the average amount you will win or lose "per hand" in any particular situation. In the case of a 16 versus an eight, if you bet $1, your expected value would be about negative 45 cents if you hit, and about negative 51 cents if you stand. The point again is, that the right play can only be determined when it is compared to the alternatives.

In the case of doubling down, it is very important not only to compare one play to its alternative, but also to use the expected value approach, rather than just seeing how often you will win. The fact is that doubling down will *never* increase your chances of winning a hand. Since you get only one card when you double down, there will be times when that card was such that you wish

---

[5]All of the percentage figures in this chapter, along with expected values, are approximate. The exact numbers depend on how many decks you are playing against and the house rules. I use these approximate figures simply to illustrate certain general concepts.

you could have taken another hit. So in many cases doubling down decreases your chances of winning.

Of course that is not always the case. For instance, if you have a

against a four showing, you would stand after you took one hit, even if you hadn't doubled down. And since 11 against a four wins about two-thirds of the time, it is quite clear that you would be very happy to double your bet. In fact, the expected value of your decision exactly doubles from about 35 cents to about 70 cents (for an original bet of $1).

The situation would be similar if you had a total of 10 against a four. Even if you couldn't double down you would still only take one card no matter what you caught. So if hitting that 10 has a positive expected value, doubling down would simply double that value.

A third hand that sometimes will take only one card whether or not doubling is allowed, is ace-six. When the dealer shows a four, five, or six, you would hit this hand one time only. And since this is also a winning situation, doubling down is clearly the better alternative than hitting, as it once again doubles your expected value.

But what about those times where a double down may result in a card that would have given you a total where the proper play would be to hit again? Doubling down on these hands decreases your chances of winning since you are no longer playing optimum strategy in those cases where you catch such a card. One obvious example is a

since you would always hit again if you caught a deuce. With a

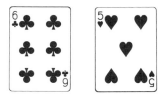

against a

a double down will force you to play less than perfectly if you catch an ace through five since you would have hit that hand again if you could have. Even doubling with an 11 against a deuce can occasionally hurt your chances since you would normally have hit again had you caught an ace.[6] Another example would be

against a

In this case a double down keeps you from hitting again as you normally would if you caught an ace or a deuce.

In spite of this, doubling down is often still correct in these situations. The reason why is that it is worth taking a small reduction in winning chances if you can bet twice as much. This is where it is important to use expected value.

For instance, I would rather bet $2 as a 58 percent shot, than $1 as a 59 percent shot. In the first case, my expected value is +32 cents (in 100 tries I expect to win $2 58 times, lose $2 42 times, and thus be ahead $32. This is an average of 32 cents per hand). In the second case it is only +18 cents.

Some type of math comes up in many of these double downs. Take that case of 11 against a nine. It has a positive expectation of about 15 cents if you do not double. But doubling is still worth it, even though you win slightly less often. The computer tells us that you do win often enough by doubling down to give you an

---

[6]I say "normally" because if the deck were positive you would stand with 12 against a deuce.

expectation of about 23 cents. When you have 11 against a deuce, your expected value is about 13 cents if you don't double down. Once again, doubling down does not double that expectation, but in this case it comes awfully close. Do you see why? It has to do with the fact that the only time doubling down hurts your strategy is specifically when you catch an ace (since the right play is to hit a 12 against a deuce). Furthermore, it's not that bad a play to stand with 12 against a deuce anyway. Thus, doubling down only slightly reduces your winning chances, and in fact, in this case your expectation would be about 22 cents, which is almost double your hitting expectation. One last example is ace-four against a four. Here, a mere hit gives you a positive expectation of 6 cents, while doubling down brings that up to about 9 cents. Once again, the expected value is not doubled because of the cards that you could catch, which would have made you want to hit again.

Now there *are* cases where doubling down, while still showing a profit, has decreased your chances of winning to the point where you do better by not doubling down. Two examples would be a

against a

or an

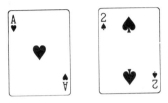

against a

A 9 against a seven wins about 59 percent of the time if you don't double down (neglecting ties), and about 53 percent of the time when you do (because of those times that you catch a small card where you should hit again, and especially when you catch a deuce and feel like throwing up). So your expected value is about 18 cents by hitting and about 12 cents by doubling. (Later on you will find that it is correct to double down with a 9 against a seven when the count is moderately positive.) In the case of ace-deuce against a four, a hit gains about 10 cents and a double down, while still positive, gains only about 7 cents.

Determining the right splitting strategies also requires thinking in terms of expected value. Once again, the idea is to compare the alternatives. And in this case, there are three alternatives: Hitting, standing, and splitting. (There may even be a fourth alternative, namely, surrendering. In one case,

against a

all four alternatives are pretty close.[7]) Note also, in the case of splitting decisions, there are a few situations where it is only right to split when the house rules allow doubling down after you split. These will be noted in the text.

There are quite a few different types of situations that can come up when you are evaluating splitting. Sometimes a split is the right play, even if it loses money, because the other two

---

[7]Standing has an expected value of minus 53 cents. Hitting also has an expected value of minus 53 cents. Surrendering , by definition, has a value of minus 50 cents. And splitting gives you two hands, each with a value of minus 24 cents. Thus, the total negative expectation for splitting is slightly better than surrendering, and is therefore, by a small margin, the correct play. (This, however, is no longer true when the deck becomes positive, as we will explain in the chapter on 16.)

alternatives are even worse. Those two eights against a ten is one example. Another is

against a

as the dealer's upcard.[8] Other times, splitting is right, even though standing makes money, because splitting makes even more. This could be true even though the two split hands don't win quite as often as the one original hand. For example,

---

[8]Hitting the 12 loses 23 cents. Splitting the sixes also loses, but not as much. That play loses either 20 cents or 12 cents, depending on whether the rules allow you to double down if you catch a good card.

against a

as the dealer's upcard.[9]

But just as in the case of doubling down, that may be okay because you are betting twice as much. Then again, it may not be okay. For instance, two nines against a seven or two tens against a five will both show a profit if you split them. However, you win so much more often if you don't, that you are better off standing.[10]

It can occur that splitting both doubles your bet and increases your chances further on each hand. This would be the case with a pair of nines against an eight showing. Here, your expected value by standing is about 6.5 cents, whereas splitting gives you two hands that each have an expected value of about 9 cents, or a total of 18 cents. (These figures assume a one-deck game where you cannot double down after splitting.)

---

[9]Standing on 18 earns about 11 cents. Splitting gives you two hands worth about 10 cents each, for a total of 20 cents.

[10]Two nines make 40 cents when you stand against a seven, but only 34 cents (17 cents on each hand) if you split. Two tens are worth 67 cents when you stay on your 20, but a total of only 50 cents when you split. Notice that you do show a profit if you split. Splitting is a sucker play, not because it loses money, but rather because it doesn't win as much in the long run as standing does. (This changes, by the way, when the deck gets moderately positive. Now both plays become correct although splitting two tens may bring "heat.")

There can even be times where splitting a hand moves you from a loser to a winner. The most extreme example is

against a

If you couldn't split them you have a negative expected value of 48 cents. When you do split them you have two hands that make you about 10 cents each. Thus, this play gains you about 68 cents. (In fact, *not* splitting two eights against a seven is the worst play you will ever see a sober person make. In terms of expected value it is worse than for instance, hitting a

against a

which is only a 48 cent mistake, as compared to the 68 cent mistake of not splitting the eights).

So far everything I have spoken of assumes a fresh deck (or multiple deck). But the fact is that this strategy, called "basic strategy," is not always the strategy that a "counter" uses. When the composition of the deck or decks have changed, it may turn out that certain plays that are normally right, become wrong and vice versa.

The point at which this happens will depend on the count. In general, the closer a decision was for a fresh deck, the quicker and the more likely you are to move to the other alternative. Standing with

against a

for instance, is not a close decision. The original difference in expected value between hitting and standing is over 25 cents. Thus, it would take an extremely strange count (very highly negative), before you would switch over to the play of hitting it. On the other hand,

against a

normally does only 2 cents better by standing, so a mildly negative deck would be enough to swing your decision to hitting in this spot.

So how does the computer determine the right strategy with various counts? (And of course, when I say count I mean "true count," as explained elsewhere.) The answer is that it goes through the same simulations as it did with an intact deck or decks. In other words, it determines for each count, the right plays all over again. For instance, the computer is asked for a new basic strategy against a true count of +3. (There is a slight fly in the ointment here because there are different ways the deck could be +3, and some of those different ways would have slightly different correct strategies attached to it. To get around this, the computer is asked to come up with the right strategy for many different types of +3 decks, and then takes a weighted average. The results are not quite perfection, but they are awfully close.)

In this book I will not bother giving you the perfect strategy for every count. Rather, I will simply use seven categories ranging from highly negative to highly positive. Rest assured that this method, besides being much easier, will cost you very little as far as your edge against the house is concerned. It might even increase your profits since you are less apt to make mistakes and will be able to play longer sessions.

Why Counting Wins

Blackjack players who keep track of the cards in some way really do have an edge over the house. That is, assuming they also play properly. The reason that's true is because merely playing the proper basic strategy, without keeping track of cards, is almost a dead even game. (It is important to give basic strategy a lot of the credit for the fact that counters have beaten casinos out of many millions of dollars. If the perfect non-counting strategy resulted in even a 2 percent disadvantage, no counter could overcome it with his knowledge of the cards. A simple change, such as paying only even money on blackjack, would do just that).

Since basic strategy is enough to get you even with the house, it is only common sense that adjusting for the cards that are out ought to swing the game to your favor. And in fact, it does. There are two reasons. One has to do with the fact that the basic strategy can sometimes be improved upon when you know something about the cards that have already been played, and thus the cards that are still in the deck. The other reason has to do with the fact that blackjack, even when you are merely playing basic strategy, sometimes offers the player an edge because of the cards left in the deck. This occurs almost half the time.[11] Of course, the other half of the time the player is at a small disadvantage. But if you are keeping track of the cards, you ought to know when you have the edge and when you don't.

The idea then, of course, is to bet more money when *you* have the edge than when the house has the edge. Thus, even though you have an edge less than half the time, *more than half of your money will be bet with an edge*. The fact is that if you know how to identify when you have an edge and you can get away with betting significantly more at those times, you will win even if you

---

[11]We are speaking of the single deck game. Multiple decks become advantageous to the player less often.

play straight basic strategy. And you will win even more if you learn to use your "count" to adjust your strategy as well as your bets.

Let us first see why certain deck compositions give the player an advantage. It has to do with the rules of the game — especially, three rules. The rules I am speaking of are the fact that:
1.   The dealer must hit up to 16, but you don't.
2.   You can double down, but he can't.
3.   You get 3-to-2 odds on a blackjack, but he doesn't.

(Three other rules that also help the counter are that you can split a pair, buy insurance when the dealer has an ace up, and surrender at some casinos.)

Since the player gets 3-to-2 odds whenever he is dealt a natural 21, it is to his advantage whenever there is a higher than usual proportion of aces and tens in the deck. You are normally dealt a blackjack about 5 percent of the time. But if the remaining cards had twice the normal proportion of aces as usual, this would raise your chances of getting a blackjack to almost 10 percent. Of course it also raises the dealer's chances of getting a blackjack, but you don't pay him 3-to-2. So if you were to be playing when the deck was this "rich" in aces you would have a very big edge. Because of this, the main idea behind counting is to identify situations where there is a higher proportion than normal of aces and tens left in the deck, and to bet more when that occurs. Just the fact that you get extra blackjacks in these situations is enough to give a player who plays properly (even simple basic strategy), an edge over the house, if most of his money is bet during these rich decks.

It turns out that decks with higher than normal proportions of tens remaining are advantageous to the player, not just because of the increased frequency of blackjacks. They also help him because the dealer will bust his stiffs more often. More importantly, the dealer will bust more often when he has a low card showing. Since the right strategy against low cards (deuce through six) showing is usually to stand with any hand above 11, you once again have a better chance of winning in these situations when the deck is rich in tens. (Notice however, that extra aces in the deck *do not* increase the dealer's chances of busting. So if the count you are using lumps aces and tens together, that adds a flaw. In fact, the first widely published count derived by Thorp only counted tens. But that also had a flaw in that it did not always identify advantageous situations correctly when the advantage or disadvantage was related to how often you would get a blackjack. As we will soon see, there is no way to get around this problem without keeping separate track of aces. But even if you don't do that, you still capture most of the advantage available to you from counting.)

As far as doubling down is concerned, it is once again true that a deck rich in tens helps the player since he normally would be quite happy to catch a ten when he doubles down. (Of course this is not the case when we are talking about soft doubling down, where catching a ten to a hand like ace-four would be a disaster.) As far as the ace is concerned, it also is a great card to have in the deck when you're doubling down, as long as you're doubling down with 9 or 10. The same is obviously not true when you have an 11, however. So once again, including aces in your count will occasionally backfire, even though overall it is to your advantage.

The above three rules are the main reason why you will have an advantage if you make bigger bets when the deck is rich in aces and tens, even if you are only sticking to basic strategy. But there is a rule that is in fact very helpful if you deviate from basic strategy advice. Basic strategy says to never buy insurance. However, that is only correct if you are *not* counting cards. If you are counting cards you should always buy insurance if there is a better than one-third chance that the dealer has a blackjack. Though the probability of the dealer having blackjack cannot be precisely known unless you are using Thorp's old-fashioned ten count, the fact is that it is usually right to take it those times that you are making bigger bets because of the rich deck. The fact that you will also make more use of the surrender rule when the deck is rich is yet another reason why you have an edge during these rich decks. (You will not only surrender more frequently, but your surrenders will occur when you have your big bets out.)

How to Count

Since *Beat the Dealer,* dozens of varying counting systems have been put forth by blackjack experts. But they all basically do the same thing. They keep track, in some way, of most or all of the cards that have been dealt in order to get a better idea of what cards are still left in the deck (or decks), the idea being that certain partial decks can be advantageous for the player, thus allowing you to get an edge by betting more when this occurs. Furthermore, you can use the information that your "count" gives you to show you those occasional times where it would be correct to deviate from the normal basic strategy. As already pointed out, extra high cards in the deck help the player, whereas extra small cards in the deck help the dealer. Again, this is because extra high cards, specifically aces and tens, make it easier to be dealt a blackjack and make it more likely that the dealer will bust when he has a low card showing. (In this second case we are speaking only of tens of course.) There are other reasons as well. Extra small cards have the opposite effect.

There are some complicated counting systems that strive to be almost perfect. Those systems take into account the fact that aces are the most important card for the player when they are still in the deck, even more important than tens, and that nines are mildly helpful to the player. They also take into account the fact that fives are the best small card as far as the dealer is concerned (since they will never bust him and often give him a very good hand).

We however will not bother with any of these more complex methods. It has been shown by many computer studies that a much simpler method will capture more than 90 percent of the edge that you could gain with one of these complicated counts. If you feel you have the time, energy, and memory to use a complex count, then be my guest. Most of them are explained in some of the books in the Recommended Reading. But for the purposes of this book we will use what is called the simple *high low count,* which was ironically introduced by Edward Thorp 35 years ago in the second edition of his book. (I say "ironically" because this count is still the preferred count of the majority of professionals even after all of these years, and even after so many slightly more accurate counts have been developed. Its ease of use has stood the test of time).

When you use the high low method to count cards you will simply be adding or subtracting one, or sometimes doing nothing at all. Before a card is dealt your count is 0. That number changes as each card comes out of the deck. The way it changes is this: You add 1 whenever you see a deuce, trey, four, five, or six. You subtract 1 whenever you see a ten or an ace. If you see a seven, eight, or nine you ignore it. That's all there is to it. The toughest thing about using this count is the fact that you have to sometimes deal with negative numbers. That may take a little practice. Thus, if your count is -5 and then you see a

and a

you're adding +2, which brings your count to -3. Do you see that?

Notice that when the count is a positive number, that is good for the player. It means that more low cards have come out than high cards. The converse is also true. When the count is a negative number it means more high cards have come out than low cards, and this is almost always bad for the player. Furthermore, the higher the count the higher your edge, and the lower the count the greater your disadvantage. However there is a very important point that needs to be made. Your advantage or disadvantage depends not only on how positive or negative your count is, but also on how many cards are still remaining to be played. *You must adjust for this.*

Blackjack pros call this adjustment *converting to the "true count."* To get the true count you divide the actual count by the approximate number of decks that have not yet been played. For instance, if you were half way through a four deck shoe and had a count of +6, the true count would be +3 since there are two decks remaining. If you had this same +6 right at the beginning of this shoe the true count would be +1½. This should be common sense. After all, seeing a few small cards at the beginning of a four or six deck shoe doesn't alter the proportion of the high to low cards very much as far as the remaining cards are concerned. Contrast this with playing against a single deck. Here, seeing a few small cards is significant. A +3 count at the beginning of a single deck game is also a true count of +3 (actually even a tad more, since there is not one full deck remaining). If your +3 is half way through a single deck the true count has actually moved up to +6. Keep in mind that the +6 is related solely to the number of unplayed decks. If you were playing an eight deck shoe and had a count of +3 after seven-and-a-half decks had been played, that would also be a true count of +6.

Throughout this book I will be using the terms *slightly positive, moderately positive,* and *highly positive,* as well as *slightly negative, moderately negative,* and *highly negative* to describe situations where you will deviate from the normal basic strategy. When I use these terms I will always be talking about the true count rather than just the count itself. Basically, slightly positive will mean about +2, moderately positive will mean about +4, and highly positive will mean about +6 or more. The same numbers will apply to my description of the negative counts.

It is not necessary that you be any more precise than that. This lack of preciseness compared to knowing the exact count for each strategy situation will cost you a negligible amount. Understand, however, that when I tell you a play which deviates from basic strategy becomes correct with, for instance, a moderately negative count, that play remains correct for a highly negative count. If I say you should, for instance, stand on

against a

when the deck is *slightly* positive, then it of course becomes the proper play against moderately or highly positive decks as well.

It will take you a few days to learn how to count even this simple high low system quickly and accurately. You must practice at home as well as in the casino. Start off by turning over one card at a time and counting down a whole deck. If you have done it correctly you are going to wind up with 0. This is because there are 20 cards that have a value of +1, and 20 cards that have a value of -1 (as well as 12 cards that have a value of 0). So when you are all done with the deck, you had better be back to 0. This is true regardless of how many decks you use in your practice sessions.

The next step is to practice two cards at a time. After awhile your brain should recognize two card combinations as simply one number. For example, a high card and a low card should just cancel out to 0 in your head. After you can quickly run through a deck two cards at a time, do it three cards at a time. Eventually three card combinations should also instantaneously become one number in your mind.

When you can easily go through any number of decks three cards at a time, it is time to practice at a casino. Bet the minimum at first because you will find it a lot more difficult to count in a casino environment than you did at home. Furthermore, don't forget that when you are playing seriously you will have to adjust your simple count to the true count by dividing your count by the approximate number of the decks remaining to be played. Your task is made more difficult because not all hands will be in neat two or three card combinations. Also, some players will bust and you need to count those cards quickly before the dealer scoops them up. Finally, other players' cards may be hard to see. If you do miss a card, just ignore it rather than lose count completely.

Once you are betting serious money it is very important that you do not lose count simply because you have a big bet riding. You cannot ever worry about any single bet, as it will never be that important in the overall scheme of things. Even if you have made a maximum bet, get dealt a pair, split it a few times, and then doubled down, you are still betting a small proportion of your total bankroll if you are gambling properly. And there is nothing you can do to alter the outcome once you have made all your correct plays. So there is no reason to lose count. The succeeding bets are just as important as this one, and that is all you should be thinking about.

A Note About Strategy Changes

As you read through this book you will notice that I will first describe the basic strategy for any particular hand. After that I will tell you when to deviate from the basic strategy. You deviate only if you are counting cards, and the count has reached a point where it is right. Sometimes it takes only a slightly abnormal count for the correct play to be other than what basic strategy recommends. In other words, it may take only a slightly positive count or a slightly negative count for you to switch strategies. For example, the basic strategy play for an

against a

is to hit. However, if the deck gets slightly positive, you should now stand.

The point I want to make here is that any time you deviate from basic strategy with a certain hand, because the deck is slightly off (either negative or positive) then you would certainly deviate if the deck is even further off in that same direction. In the case of 12 against a trey, when I say to stand if the deck is slightly positive, you should realize that this also means that you should stand if the deck is moderately or highly positive as well. In other words when I recommend a strategy change at a certain degree of positiveness or negativeness, that is merely the point at which you *begin* to make that particular change. So when I say to hit

against a

when the deck gets moderately negative, I also mean to hit it when the deck is highly negative, but *not* when it is merely slightly negative. (And of course you should not hit if the deck is neutral or positive either.)

Insurance

I assume that most of you know the rules of blackjack. For those who don't I include an Appendix at the back of the book that explains the game and the options available to you. But I would like to say something right here about two of those options. One is "insurance" and the other is "surrender." Surrender will be discussed in the next chapter.

Both insurance and surrender are offered by casinos in the hopes that you will use these options incorrectly. Most do. But good players only use these options when it is to their advantage to do so.

Insurance is offered whenever the dealer has an ace showing (before she has checked to see whether she has a blackjack). If you want to buy insurance, you put up an amount up to half of the size of your original bet. If the dealer does have a blackjack she will pay you 2-to-1 odds on this extra bet of yours. Thus, if you have taken it for the full amount you wind up pushing on the whole deal. She takes your original bet, but the 2-to-1 odds on the side bet exactly make up for it. (If you happen to have a blackjack when the dealer shows an ace, buying insurance will guarantee you a payoff of exactly the size of your original bet, regardless of whether she has blackjack or not. Do you see why?)

The key thing to understand here is that insurance is truly a *side bet*. It really isn't insurance at all. Some players think it is smart to "insure" their best hands since that will keep them from losing to a blackjack while giving them a good chance to wind up with a ½ bet profit. But they are simply wrong.

When you buy insurance you are taking 2-to-1 odds on something that is normally greater than 2-to-1. That costs you money. Period. Four out of thirteen cards are tens. The odds against a particular card being a ten are therefore 9-to-4 or 2¼-to-1. And when you buy insurance you are simply betting that the dealer's hole card is a ten. And you are getting 2-to-1 on something that is usually at least 2.2-to-1. If you took insurance every time it was offered you would have about a 7 percent disadvantage on that bet.

The only time it is right to take insurance is if at least one-third of the remaining unseen cards are tens. So you have to be counting to ever consider doing it. If you play mere basic strategy you should *never* buy insurance. If you are counting, whether you buy insurance has everything to do with your count and nothing to do with your total. Basically you buy insurance whenever the true count is moderately positive. This criteria is not perfect unless you are using the ten count, but it will give you the right advice the vast majority of the time.

Surrender

One option that is offered by a few casinos is something they call *surrender*.[12] The idea is that you can pay the house half of your bet rather than go through with your hand. So for instance if you bet $100, are dealt a

and the dealer shows a

you can opt to lose 50 bucks before you draw any cards or see the dealer's hand.

The reason why casinos offer this option is that most people do not use it properly. In fact, most people who do surrender at all tend to surrender too much. It is only correct to surrender if the expected value of your normal play is worse than negative 50 cents per $1 bet. That does not come up very often.

---

[12]Even though I say "a few casinos" the surrender option has become more common during the past few years, so be on the lookout for it.

For instance, let's take the case of a

versus a

If you stand, as you should, you will win 35 percent of the time. Does this mean you are better off surrendering? Well, if you played 100 such hands for $1 each, you would find yourself winning 35 and losing 65. Thus you would be down $30 after 100 hands. Had you surrendered each time instead it would have cost you 50 cents per hand for a total of $50 after those 100 hands.

It turns out that in order for surrendering to be correct you must win *less than 25 percent of the hands*. (This figure assumes that there cannot be ties. When ties are possible it changes the math slightly.) There are a few cases where your expected value is slightly worse than negative 50 cents (16 against a nine, ten, or an ace, and 15 against a ten). But it is so close that there is very little to be gained by surrendering in these spots. However, those numbers assume a neutral deck. Once the deck gets rich in tens, these and other situations are quite a bit worse than negative 50 cents and thus that surrender option becomes a lot more valuable to the counter. This is especially true if you are using a big bet spread (as you might in a shoe game).

There is one type of surrender that can be incredibly advantageous. Pros call it *early surrender*. Normally casinos will not let you surrender before they check to see whether they have a blackjack under their ace or ten. That is called late surrender, and that is what I am assuming is available as far as this book is concerned. Atlantic City, however, once offered early surrender (and it has occurred for brief periods of time at other casinos). This cost them tens of millions of dollars. The reason why is that there are many situations where your expected value is far worse than negative 50 cents when there is still a possibility that the dealer may have a blackjack. This is true against a ten showing but especially true against an ace showing. Just playing basic strategy, including proper early surrender strategy, gives the player about a half a percent edge. The basic strategy for early surrender is to do it against an ace with a 12 through 17, as well as 6 and 7, and to do it against a ten with a 14, 15, and 16. With a positive count you would add a few more hands. It is unlikely that you will ever find a game like this, but if you do, you must sit down and play right after you call me.

Part Two

The Totals

The Totals

Introduction

What follows is a totally different way to explain proper blackjack strategy. There are no charts and no "index" numbers. (That means I will not give you a precise count at which to make a particular play.)

What I will be doing instead is simply talking to you about each total. I will tell you the basic strategy for those totals and when to deviate from the basic strategy because of the count. Often I will try to give you a common sense rationale for many of those plays (though the bottom line is that you do them because that is what the computer says). This ought to make them a lot easier to learn and memorize.

Occasionally I will digress into other gambling topics that are brought to mind by the proper play of a particular total. These digressions will also hopefully make the subject more interesting than more charts and thus easier to learn.

The chapters range from "A Total of 21" to "A Total of 2." They include all hands that add up to these numbers, including soft hands and pairs. Aces count as 11 in soft hands (so the chapters on 2 and 3 are actually superfluous). Thus, for instance, the chapter titled "A Total of 18" discusses ace-seven (or ace-four-trey, etc), and a pair of nines, as well as regular hard 18.

A Total of 21

Discussion

Is there anything to say about a total of 21? You stand and you collect your money, unless the dealer ties you. Well, actually there are some things to say. The first has to do with hands like

your natural 21s, otherwise known as blackjacks.[13] There is one decision that will often come up when you have blackjack, and that is whether to buy insurance. In general, you do not buy insurance unless the deck is moderately positive. However, in the case where you are dealt a blackjack, it is often said that this is one time you buy insurance regardless of the count. The reason they say that is because buying insurance guarantees you a win. For instance, if you bet $10 and are dealt a blackjack and proceed to spend $5 on insurance, you now are certain to win exactly $10. This is because you will either get paid $15 on your blackjack and lose your $5 insurance bet, or push on your blackjack and get paid $10 on your insurance bet.

In spite of this argument *you should not buy insurance.* The reason, without going into detailed mathematics is simply that you are better off taking the $15 pay, when it is coming to you and taking the push the remaining times. Against a normal deck you

---

[13]They are also sometimes referred to as naturals or snappers.

will get that $15 a little bit more than two-thirds of the time. So your average pay will be a little bit more than $10. Of course, you should buy insurance if the deck is moderately positive, just like with any other total. But since your hand contains a ten, don't forget to take that into account before you make a decision. (This concept of counting the cards in your own hand for insurance purposes is even more important when you are dealt a hand like

consisting of two tens. That hand is even less likely to be right to insure [because it contains two tens]. Thus ironically, your bad hands should be "insured" more often than good hands.)[14]

I am going to use the 21 total to illustrate another interesting mathematical principle. Might it ever be worth it to *double down* with a soft 21? First, let's look at the case where it is not a blackjack.[15] Might this actually be worth doubling when the deck is positive? To show why that is unlikely you really don't need a computer, but rather just a little bit of common sense. If we assume your 21 is a win, and we eliminate ties from the

---

[14]You may want to pass on insuring some of your bad hands when the deck is only moderately positive. The reason for this is that only counters make this play and it can be a tipoff to the pit. However, you are giving up too much if you neglect to insure if the count is highly positive.

[15]Either because the casino will let you double down on three or more cards or because you have split aces and caught a ten at one of those rare casinos that will let you double down on that hand.

computation, the fact is that doubling down on soft 21 is risking three bets to win one. Can you see why?

If the double down is successful it adds one bet to your win, but if it fails it costs you three bets (not two), because you lose your double bet *plus* the one you would have won. Therefore, this play would have to work in the neighborhood of 75 percent of the time (again, ignoring ties) for it to be worth doing.

To see if you followed my method, let's analyze the play of doubling down with blackjack. How often would this have to work before it would be right to do? (I realize I am kind of straying from the subject of how to play blackjack here, but I will be making similar comments throughout the book whenever a particular total might bring up an important gambling idea that I think would be helpful to you.) See if you can do this problem yourself before you read on.

Again the general technique involves comparing your possible gain to your possible loss. Since you had a one and a half win guaranteed, a double down, which gives up that one and a half bets, can only gain you an extra half of a bet. If, on the other hand, your play backfires, you have cost yourself a total of three and one-half bets. You are laying 3½-to-½ or 7-to-1. In other words, you would have to be more than a 7-to-1 favorite to make it right. Obviously that does not ever figure to come up, so stand on your blackjacks.

Bottom Line

Basic Strategy

Hard 21: Always stand.

Soft 21 or a natural: Always stand.

If You Are Counting

Hard 21: Always stand.

Soft 21 or a natural: Always stand.

A Total of 20

Discussion

Obviously,

is an excellent hand and, under normal conditions you would never think of doing anything other than standing with it. And that is of course, what basic strategy says to do. However, 20 is often a pair of tens such as

and bad blackjack players are known to split them against upcards such as a five or a six. They are wrong to do that, but it is important to understand that splitting tens is not a losing play. Rather, it is a bad play. There is a difference. If you split two tens every time you got them, you would be ahead money for those hands. The problem is that you would be ahead even more money if you didn't split the two tens. This is a very important gambling concept that applies not only to many blackjack decisions, but to all kinds of general gambling decisions. What makes a play right or wrong is not simply whether or not it makes money, but rather

51

how it does compared to the alternatives. Getting back to 20, another play that would show a profit is doubling down on

Once again, however, you would show an even greater profit if you didn't.

All the above, however, applies to the basic strategy. The fact is that it can be occasionally right to split two tens and to double with an ace-nine. You do it against a five or a six if the deck is moderately positive, and against a four when the deck is highly positive. However, there is a reason not to do it, even under these circumstances. The reason is that splitting tens or doubling on ace-nine can mark you as being a "counter." So you have to decide whether pushing a small edge is worth the heat it might bring down on you.

Bottom Line

Basic Strategy

Hard 20: Always stand.

Soft 20: Always stand.

Pair of Tens: Never split, always stand.

If You Are Counting

Hard 20: Always stand.

Soft 20: Double against a five or six when the deck gets moderately positive. Double against a four when the deck gets highly positive.

Pair of Tens: Split against a five or six when the deck gets moderately positive. Split against a four when the deck gets highly positive.

A Total of 19

Discussion

This is a pretty simple one. Basically, you just stand. Sure, the dealer may have a 20, but no sane person should ever hit a hard

unless they are cheating. However, a soft

may be a profitable double down. The basic strategy play is to simply stand. However you do double down with ace-eight against a five or a six once the deck becomes just slightly positive. And you would double against a trey or a four if the deck is moderately positive.

Bottom Line

Basic Strategy

Hard 19: Always stand.

Soft 19: Always stand.

If You Are Counting

Hard 19: Always stand.

Soft 19: Never just hit. Double down against five or six when the deck gets slightly positive. Double down against trey or four when the deck gets moderately positive.

A Total of 18

Discussion

There is quite a bit to say about a total of 18. Not the "hard" variety of course. With that hand you would simply stand no matter what the dealer was showing. It's not a great hand, and if you were dealt it every time you would break about even. But as long as the dealer shows an eight or lower you have a positive expectation. Your negative expectation comes from those times the dealer has a nine, ten, or ace showing. In any case, there is nothing you can do about it except stand and hope.

However, the other two kinds of eighteen namely "soft"

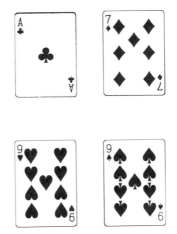

and

are both very interesting hands. With the soft 18, there are three different things you may do: Hit, stand, or double down. Though the average player routinely stands with this hand, the only times you should normally do this is when the dealer shows a seven, eight, or deuce.

When the dealer shows a nine or ten the basic strategy play is to hit it. This may seem to go against common sense since there are only three cards you can catch which will make you happy and six cards which will make you sad (four cards, namely the tens, will keep you at 18). In spite of this the computer says you must gamble. This is because when you catch one of those three cards, ace, deuce, or trey, you help yourself much more than you hurt yourself when you catch a bad card. Notice that when you do catch a bad card you would hit again, except of course when you catch a nine, which gives you a hard 17.

Interestingly, it is even more important that you hit the soft 18 against a nine than against a ten. The logic is similar to why it is more important that you hit stiffs against a seven than against a ten, which we discuss further in the chapter on 16. It comes down to risk versus reward. There is a greater reward when you do catch an ace or deuce when you are up against a nine. In fact, the play of hitting soft 18 against a ten is rather close and you should stop doing it when the deck becomes slightly positive. Not so against a nine. Against an ace, whether you should hit or stand is so close that the right strategy depends on the house rules. And you would definitely stand once the deck got even slightly positive. In fact, any hit of soft 18 can bring on some scrutiny from the pit, as this play is one of the hallmarks of a good player. Thus you may want to consider standing just for the sake of deception.

As for doubling down, doing it with soft 18 can be a definite gainer. Unlike soft 17, the play doesn't quite double your expectation because you would not hit it if you couldn't double down, as you would with

So doubling down forces you to play slightly incorrectly. However, notice that against a small card if you did hit an ace-seven you would almost always stand no matter what you caught (the only exception would be if you caught a four and the dealer was showing a trey). The bottom line is that doubling with an ace-seven against all small cards except a deuce significantly increases your expectation, and thus you do it against a trey through six.

The count can of course change these strategies. For one thing, you would double down against a deuce once the count got positive. On the other hand, you would no longer double down against a trey when the deck was at all negative. Against a four, five, or six you need a very negative deck to not double down. Of course, if you were at a casino that does not allow doubling down on these hands, you would simply stand against all of these small cards regardless of the count.

Now we come to a pair of nines. This is my favorite pair. When someone tells you that they are an expert blackjack player just ask them when they split nines. If they get it right you can believe them, but few get it right. Still the fact is that the right play should be pretty much common sense. For instance, splitting nines against a ten or an ace is obviously wrong. Why would you double your bet when the nineteens you are trying to make are still quite likely to lose?

But what about against a nine? Though all strategies are eventually determined by computer, not just by logical reasoning, the fact is that a little logic should lead you to the conclusion that this is a proper split. If you stand on that 18 you are in trouble when the dealer shows that nine. He will often have 19. Notice that if he does, splitting will do no worse than standing if you catch a ten on either of the nines. Often you will do even better than this, so it is worth risking the possibility of losing two bets.

Similar reasoning applies when the dealer shows an eight. Now you are likely to push by standing, while splitting will occasionally cost you two bets. But once again, if you catch even one ten you do at least as well as standing would have if the dealer had an 18. And you could easily win two bets. The bottom line is you do quite a bit better in the long run by splitting.

What about against a seven? Here the situation is a little different. The reason why is that your 18 is already in excellent shape. It's sort of like a

against a

In both cases splitting makes money, but standing makes even more in the long run.

As far as playing your nines against a small card, the idea here is to split to get "more money in the pot." Each of the two individual nines don't earn quite as much as your 18, but combined they earn more. Thus you split two nines against a deuce through six.

As far as how you adjust to the count, it goes like this. (Remember that you are somewhat quicker to split when you can double down after splitting. The following advice assumes you can't.) While it is never right to split nines against a ten, it can be right against an ace. Don't forget that you only split *after* the dealer has already *checked for blackjack*.[16] Because of that, it is

---

[16]Some casinos do not check for blackjack until the hand is over. At most of those places they will refund extra money lost

right to split when the deck is moderately positive. It is also right to split those nines against a seven when the deck becomes moderately positive. As for *refraining* from the basic strategy play of splitting, you would do this with at least a slightly negative deck against a deuce or trey, a moderately negative deck against a four, five, or six, and with a very negative deck you would no longer split against an eight or nine. (Remember, by the way, that when you are counting you may deviate from basic strategy after you split. For instance, if you split the nines against a six when the deck is mildly negative you should hit if you catch a three. This is because the deck was not negative enough to stop you from splitting, but was negative enough to start you hitting a 12 against a six. This concept of course comes up all the time in splitting decisions.)

Bottom Line

Basic Strategy

Hard 18: Always stand.

Soft 18: Hit against nine or ten. Stand against deuce, seven, and eight. Double against a trey through six. (If you can't double, stand.)

Pair of nines: Split against everything *except* seven, ten, or ace.

If You Are Counting

Hard 18: Always stand

---

due to splits or double downs when they do have a natural. So your strategy doesn't change. Those casinos that don't give this refund should not be patronized.

Soft 18: Start hitting against an ace (as well as against a nine or ten) when the deck gets slightly negative. Double against a deuce (as well as against trey through six) when the deck gets slightly positive. Stop doubling against a trey when the deck gets slightly negative. Stop doubling against a four through six when the deck gets very negative.

Pair of nines: Start splitting against a seven and an ace when the deck gets moderately positive. Stop splitting against deuce or trey when the deck gets slightly negative. Stop splitting against a four, five, or six when the deck gets moderately negative. Stop splitting against an eight or nine when the deck gets highly negative.

A Total of 17

Discussion

is a terrible hand. We all know that. And the mathematicians agree. If you were dealt a 17 every time you would get completely destroyed. Against a high card, it costs you more, on average, than 30 cents per dollar bet. Even against a low card, you lose about a dime. In spite of this, you must stand, since hitting would fare even worse. There is one interesting exception. It is against an ace. It turns out that the mathematically correct play is to hit a hard seventeen when the dealer has an ace showing, and the deck is highly negative. This actually makes sense since the dealer will almost never bust with such a deck, and simultaneously your chances of making a better hand have improved. However I do not recommend this play since it might draw attention to yourself. (Also, if the deck is this highly negative, you might be better off taking a break.)

is not nearly as bad. But never even think about standing on it, even if you are not allowed to double down. The fact that a hit might hurt your hand does not nearly make up for the fact that you will probably improve and that a 17, as we have already said, loses lots of money when you stand on it. It is true that your first hit will more likely harm you than help you since there are five bad cards to catch and four good ones (and four more that leave you with that same total of 17). But that doesn't matter. Against a high card you will hit again those five times that you catch badly and some of those times will work out okay. This means that you are more likely to improve than to bust. Against a low card you will probably not hit again when you catch a small card, but the harm you do is small, whereas you gain quite a lot those four times you do catch something nice. One way to practically prove that hitting soft 17 is always better than standing is by alluding to the fact that those casinos that ask their dealers to hit the hand add to their house edge.

When you do hit soft 17, what you do next depends on the dealer's upcard (and the count, if you are counting). For instance, against a nine, you would hit again if you caught an ace as well as a five, six, seven, eight, or nine. Against a four, you would stand no matter what you caught. Against a deuce, you would hit again only if you caught a five. These examples assume you are playing basic strategy or that you are counting, but the count doesn't indicate a non-basic strategy play.

When allowed, ace-six can be an advantageous double down. Notice that against a four, five, or six you would take only one card even if you couldn't double down. In other words, you would stand no matter what you caught. This means that doubling down totally doubles your expected value against these upcards, since the play does not reduce your chances of winning. As an example, against a five your expected value is 10 cents per dollar bet if you hit, and therefore 20 cents if you double down. That's a 10 cent gain.

Against a deuce or trey the double down is not nearly as strong. There are two reasons for this. Number one is that the hand is not as valuable to start with. Number two is that doubling down doesn't completely double your expectation since you might catch a five and wish you could have hit again. Basic strategy tells you not to double down against a deuce, but there is a slight gain against a trey. So the basic strategy with ace-six is to double down, if allowed, against trey, four, five, and six.

If you are counting you would also double down against a deuce if the count got at all positive. On the other hand, you would not double down against a trey once the deck got somewhat negative. To stop doubling down against four, five, or six the deck would need to be highly negative.

Bottom Line

Basic Strategy

Hard 17: Always stand.

Soft 17: Hit against a deuce as well as seven through ace. Double against a trey through six. (If you can't double, hit.)

If You Are Counting

Hard 17: Hit against an ace if the deck gets highly negative.

Soft 17: Start doubling down against a deuce as well as the trey through six if the deck gets even slightly positive. Stop doubling down against a trey if the deck gets slightly negative. Stop doubling down against a four through six if the deck gets highly negative.

A Total of 16

Discussion

If you are dealt a

you will naturally get sick. And there is not too much I can tell you to make you feel better. That total has no greater chance of winning when you stand than a 12 does, yet it has a far better chance of busting if you hit. But when you are dealt a 16, there is little time to feel sorry for yourself. In fact, if you are a counter it is extremely important that you don't. Because with a 16 you often have to change your decision based on your count. That doesn't mean that your expertise will give you a good chance of winning the hand. All it means is that you might be able to increase your chances by 1 or 2 percent, but your chances will still be lousy. However, from the standpoint of your end result, a 1 or 2 percent increase is just as important when it moves your chances from 25 to 27 percent as when it moves it from 62 to 64 percent. So be just as focused when you're dealt a 16 as when you are dealt an 11.

The basic strategy for hard 16 is pretty simple. You stand against a deuce through six, and you hit when the dealer shows seven through ace. Even most beginners stand on 16 against small cards. It is a terrible play to do otherwise. Against a deuce, hitting is about a 17 cent mistake for every dollar bet, and it would be worse against the other small cards. That's not to say that you will probably win if you stand, far from it. But if you hit you are even more likely to lose. In a similar vein, you *hit* your 16s against high cards not because you will probably win, but simply because you will more likely win. For instance against a nine, you will win about 23 percent of the time if you stand and about 26 percent of the time if you hit. Similar numbers apply to all of the dealer upcards from seven through ace.

Many beginning blackjack players hit 16 against the dealer's ten, but not against the dealer's seven. They reason that a ten is stronger than a seven, and thus it is more important to hit against that card. You, of course, will not make this mistake since you will be religiously following the advice in this book. But what makes this error on the part of the beginners particularly interesting is that they have it backwards. It is a much worse mistake to stand against a seven than against a ten. Can you see why? It involves a rather important concept that comes up often in blackjack, as well as other gambling games.

That concept is balancing risks versus rewards. Against either a ten or a seven you take the same high risk of busting when you hit that 16. However, against a seven the reward for that risk is much greater. The reason why, of course, is that when you do catch a small card your chances of winning are greater against the seven (since he often has 17) than it is against the ten (since he often has 20). In purely mathematical terms, hitting 16 against a ten moves you from a 54 cent loser to a 52 cent loser. But against a seven, your hit moves you from a 48 cent loser to a 40 cent loser. So these numbers confirm that you gain more by hitting against a seven than against a ten.

There is one other basic strategy play that you may use when you have a hard 16. I am speaking of *surrender*. Remember, we just said that hitting a 16 against a ten costs you 52 cents for every dollar bet in the long run. Well, if you surrender you lose only 50 cents, thus saving 2 cents. So if you're at a casino that allows surrender, the basic strategy play with 16 is to do it against a ten, and also an ace.

Now let's talk about how you may change your strategy with 16 based on the count. First of all, let's continue with the subject of surrender. The deck has to be at least neutral to make it right. Once the deck gets mildly negative no hand should be surrendered. However, when the deck gets positive you should surrender more often. Hands other than 16 should be surrendered, as we will get to shortly. 16 itself should be surrendered against a nine when the deck is mildly positive, and against an eight when the deck is highly positive. (Exception: A pair of eights, which we will come to shortly.)

As far as your hitting and standing strategies are concerned, it is extremely unlikely that you would ever consider hitting a 16 against a small card. It can be right against a deuce or a trey when the deck is extremely negative, but this is such a rare occurrence that you shouldn't even worry about it. On the other hand, it is quite likely that you will change your basic strategy with 16 when the dealer shows a high card, especially a ten. It turns out that if the deck is at all positive you should stand with that sixteen, *but only if you cannot surrender*. (In fact, any time throughout this book that I tell you to stand on a stiff against a high card with a certain count, it would be better if you could surrender instead.)

Some of you may wonder why a higher count means that it is better to stand with a 16 against a ten. Since a higher count indicates more big cards in the deck, it also means that the dealer is more likely to have a good hand. Might not that make up for the fact that a higher count makes it more likely for you to bust? Though this is a good question, it turns out that the answer is no. Your increased chances of busting with a higher count is more important than your increased chances of facing a good hand. Thus, you stand.

However, this question does illustrate a weakness in typical counting methods. The weakness has to do with the fact that high cards may give you both a reason to hit and to stand, depending on whether that high card is coming off to you or whether that high card is in the dealer's hole. Notice that in the particular case of 16 against a ten, the *six* alone escapes this schizophrenia. Extra sixes in the deck are a double reason to stand. They bust you if you catch them, and they give the dealer a 16 if he has one of those sixes in the hole. Sadly, counting systems almost always treat sixes as low cards, which is just the opposite of what you would want in this particular situation. Not that you can do much about this problem. Fives also are somewhat misrepresented by regular counts when the dealer has sixteen against a ten. Extra fives in the deck are a big reason to hit because catching one of them beats the dealer even if he has his often made 20. In fact, Peter Griffin has shown that when playing a single deck your strategy decisions would more likely be correct if you use this simple rule "hit 16 against a ten if there are more sixes left in the deck than fives," than if you used the normal count to make your decision. However, all that being said, there is little that you can do about these inherent problems unless you are playing a single deck game and have a photographic memory. Anyway, just remember to stand on 16 against a ten when the count is at all positive, and against a nine when it is highly positive, as long as you can't surrender instead.

Now let us consider

Clearly, if you can't double down, you should never stand. If you can't see this you may as well return this book right now. If you do hit the hand, what you do next depends on the card you catch. It reverts to the basic strategy for other totals. For instance if you catch an ace you would hit it again, no matter what the dealer shows. If you caught a trey you would always stand. If you caught a seven you would hit against a high card, but not a low card. If you caught a deuce you would hit against a nine, ten, or ace. And if you caught a six you would hit against everything but four, five, or six. Of course we are talking basic strategy here. Sometimes the count would alter these plays.

At those casinos that allow you to double down on a soft16, you would do it against a four, five, and six. Doubling down with this hand does not quite double your expectation as compared to hitting. This is because you must stand when you catch an ace, which is something you wouldn't do had you not doubled down. Still it is the right play against these three upcards. If the count got moderately high you should also double down against a trey. On the other hand, if it got moderately negative you should stop doubling down against a four.

The last kind of 16 is

There is a frequent expression heard among blackjack players that says, "always split aces and eights." It turns out that this expression is correct, at least as far as basic strategy is concerned. It is pretty obvious why you should usually split two eights. Not only are you giving yourself two decent starting hands, you are also breaking up the dreaded 16. As I already mentioned, *not* splitting them against a seven is the worst mistake in blackjack.

The only time it is not obvious that splitting eights is right is when the dealer shows a nine, a ten, or an ace. In these cases many players are reluctant to split since there is a good chance they will now lose two bets rather than one. They are right to be unhappy, but they are wrong not to split. Though both of the eights will lose money, the combined losses will be less than the one 16 would lose in the long run. And you must think of the long run. If you don't have the courage to make this play, you shouldn't be playing at all. However, if you are counting cards the situation may change.

If the deck is moderately positive you would no longer split against a ten. There is just too much chance you would lose a double bet. But keep in mind that if you don't split you should now stand because you stand on 16 against a ten with positive decks. Actually, the even more preferred play is to surrender, since that is the even better play with 16 against ten when the deck is at all positive. The same can be said when the dealer shows an ace, except now you need only a slightly positive deck to not split. However in the case of an ace, that slightly positive deck, while enough to keep you from splitting, is not enough to keep you from hitting. So if you can't surrender, you still hit.

As far as other upcards are concerned, no normal count will stop you from splitting eights. (Exception: You do stop splitting eights against an ace if the deck is slightly negative, but only against games where the dealer hits soft 17. When the dealer stands on soft 17 your two eights go way up in value for obvious reasons). The only thing you might do is adjust your subsequent strategy. For instance, if the deck was moderately negative you would not double down if you caught a deuce to one of your eights, and the dealer was showing an eight. Likewise, if you caught a five to one of your eights you would hit again with a moderately negative count if the dealer showed a trey.

16 is probably the most complicated number to talk about. If you got through this chapter, you now have smooth sailing.

Bottom Line

Basic Strategy

Hard 16: Hit versus seven through ace. (Surrender against an ace or ten if you can.) Stand versus deuce through six.

Soft 16: Double if you can against four through six. (Hit otherwise.)

Pair of eights: Split against all upcards.

If You Are Counting

Hard 16: Stand against a ten when the deck gets slightly positive. (If you can't surrender.) Surrender against a nine when the deck gets slightly positive. Stand against a nine when the deck gets highly positive. (If you can't surrender.) Surrender against an eight when the deck gets highly positive. Hit against a deuce when the deck gets highly negative. Stop surrendering totally when the deck gets at all negative

Soft 16: Never stand. Start doubling against a trey if the deck gets moderately positive. Stop doubling against a four if the deck gets moderately negative.

Pair of eights: Stop splitting against a ten if the deck is moderately positive. Surrender if you can; otherwise stand.

A Total of 15

Discussion

may seem almost as lousy as

But the fact is that hitting it busts you immediately only about seven out of thirteen times, rather than the eight out of thirteen times for 16. So it is not really quite as bad. Still the basic strategy is the same. You would hit it against a seven through ace, and stand otherwise. Against a small card your best chance is still that the dealer goes broke. Against a high card, however, you have a significantly better chance by hitting.

It is also correct to surrender a 15 against a ten, but it is extremely close. If there is any heat on you at all you are better off not drawing attention to yourself and should just go ahead and hit it. If you are counting you should hit a 15 against a deuce or a trey if the deck is highly negative. As for when you should stand with a 15 against a high card, the only time that is right using typical counts is when the deck is highly positive and the dealer shows a ten. Of course in this case you would be much better off surrendering. (In fact, it is correct to surrender 15 against a nine with a moderately positive deck.)

If you somehow knew that there were a lot of extra sevens in the deck you would be right not to hit against a nine, everything else being equal. That seven is what I call a *key* card because it busts you but could give the dealer a total of 16. But that is simply a fine point that is interesting to know but is not necessary to use for your blackjack success.

As for soft 15, you should double down with this hand against a four, five, or six. If you are counting you would stop doubling against a four if the deck was slightly negative and stop doing it against a five if the deck was moderately negative.

Bottom Line

Basic Strategy

Hard 15: Hit versus seven through ace. (Surrender against a ten if you can.) Stand versus deuce through six.

Soft 15: Double if you can against four, five, or six.

If You Are Counting

Hard 15: Start standing against a ten (if you can't surrender) when the deck gets moderately positive. Surrender against a nine when the deck gets moderately positive. Hit against a deuce or trey when the deck gets highly negative.

Soft 15: Stop doubling against a four when the deck gets slightly negative. Stop doubling against a five when the deck gets moderately negative.

A Total of 14

Hitting an

will not bust you as often as hitting a

or a

however, you still bust often enough that you are better off hoping the dealer goes over when he shows a small card rather than taking the chance yourself. Thus, the basic strategy play remains the same as it does for the two aforementioned totals. Namely, you hit against a seven through ace and stand against a deuce through six.

What does change is the point at which you deviate from that strategy according to the count. For instance, against a deuce or a trey, you now need the deck to get only *moderately* negative for it to be right to hit that 14. The totals of 15 and 16 require *highly* negative counts. With a 14 a highly negative count would indicate a hit against everything, even a four, five, or six. On the other hand, 14 improves often enough by hitting that you would in fact hit against high cards regardless of the count. This is once again different than your strategy for a 15 or a 16 where you will sometimes stand against high cards when the deck is positive enough.

There is, however, one well known exception. It occurs when you have 14, the dealer has a ten showing, and there are little or no sevens left in the deck. When this happens it is right to stand even against an otherwise neutral count.

The reason has to do with my "key card concept," explained earlier. In the case of 14 against a ten, the seven is the one non-schizophrenic card. Every other card has one effect if it is coming out to you and a different effect if it is in the dealer's hole. The seven however, is a doubly good card to be in the deck if you do hit your hand. That is because the seven makes you 21 if you hit, while simultaneously making the dealer an easily beatable total of 17 if he has it in the hole.

On the other side of the coin, an absence of sevens in the deck makes hitting much less enticing. You won't snag a 21, plus if you hit something like a trey or four you may still lose. Thus you are better off standing and hoping the dealer has a small card in the hole and goes on to bust. The effect of the seven in this particular situation is so strong that the *basic strategy* for one deck is to *stand* with two sevens against a ten simply because that particular 14 includes half the sevens in the deck. Still I only mention this for the sake of completeness. I do not expect that you will be keeping separate track of sevens, and even if you were it would be rare that a situation would arise where it would be right to stand with a 14 against a 10. We will get back to two sevens shortly when we discuss splitting strategy.

is of course a total with which you would never stand. Thus, the only question is whether to hit or to double down (keeping in mind that there are many casinos that will not let you double down with this hand). If you do simply hit, the main thing to remember is that you revert to proper strategy for whatever new total you achieve. Thus if the dealer is showing a nine, you would hit a second time unless your first hit was a five, six, or seven. If the dealer was showing a deuce you would hit a second time if your first hit was an ace, deuce, trey, or eight. (Do you see why?) Of course, that might change based on the count.

As far as doubling down is concerned, you gain a little bit of expected value (even though you reduce your win chances somewhat) if you double down against a five or a six. If the deck is at all positive you should also double down against a four. On the other hand, you should not double down at all once the deck is mildly negative.

Now lets get back to

The proper strategy for this particular pair is very similar to the proper strategy for a pair of deuces, treys, and sixes. Basic strategy for two sevens is to split them when the dealer shows a deuce, trey, four, five, or six. This is true even if you cannot double down after splitting, even though the strategy for other pairs would change depending on that rule.

As far as counting is concerned, the correct *splitting* strategy for two sevens is once again not susceptible to changes in the count. However the count might enter into things. For instance, if you split two sevens and caught a six against a trey showing, you would hit it again if the deck was slightly negative.

Bottom Line

Basic Strategy

Hard 14: Hit against seven through ace; otherwise stand.

Soft 14: Double against five or six.

Pair of sevens: Split against four through seven.

If You Are Counting

Hard 14: Surrender against a ten if the deck is moderately positive. Hit versus a deuce if the deck gets moderately negative. Hit versus trey or a four if the deck gets highly negative.

Soft 14: Double against a four when the deck gets moderately positive. Stop doubling at all when the deck is slightly negative

Pair of sevens: Stick with basic strategy regardless of the count.

A Total of 13

Discussion

From the standpoint of basic strategy,

works just like those other stiffs above it (16, 15, and 14). In other words, you hit against a big card, seven through ace, and you stand against a small card, deuce through six. However, because of the fact that taking a hit will bust you less than 40 percent of the time, it is not that rare that the count will indicate you should do it, even against a small card. This is, of course, especially true when the dealer shows a deuce or a trey. In fact, if the deck is even the tiniest bit negative, you should hit a 13 against a deuce. A slightly negative deck also would change your strategy to hitting a 13 against a trey. Against a four, five, or six the deck would have to reach the moderately negative range before you would hit that 13.

As far as *not* hitting a 13 against a high card, for all intents and purposes it should never be done. The only possible exception would be if you were playing against a single deck and you somehow knew that almost every seven and eight had already been played. Once again, this is related to my "key card concept," explained in my book, *Getting the Best of It*. If this was the situation there would be almost no chance of improving to 20 or 21, and little reason to try to improve to a lesser hand, since the dealer is very unlikely to have 17 or 18. This situation of course can never be uncovered if you are using a normal count, and in any case could only reasonably be expected to occur against one deck. Thus, for all practical purposes, you should always hit a hard 13 against any high card.

should always at least be hit. In casinos where you can double-down it is sometimes the right play. Notice, however, that doubling with ace-deuce is not as favorable as some other soft double-downs. The reason has to do with the fact that you will more frequently catch a card where you would like to have hit again. For instance, if the dealer is showing five and you double-down you will be sorry that option was available if you catch anywhere from an ace to a four (not to mention a nine or a ten).

Contrast this with

against a

In this case you would only take one card, even if you couldn't double-down. Nothing that you caught would make you hit again. Thus, whatever your positive expectation is with the ace-six, it doubles when you double-down. Such is not the case with an ace-deuce. Notice further that even a hand like

gains more from doubling than ace-deuce does, since the only card you could catch to make you hit again would be another ace. Still, with all that being said, you do gain a tiny bit (basic strategy wise) by doubling-down with an ace-deuce against a five or six.

As far as the count changing that strategy, there is no question that an even slightly bad deck would make this play a horribly bad play. This is just common sense, since not only would extra small cards help the dealer, but they would make it that much more likely that you yourself will catch a card that would make you want to hit your hand again.

The converse, however, is not true. A highly positive deck, which normally is a big indicator toward doubling-down (with totals like 9 or 10), really doesn't give that much extra incentive when you have an ace-deuce, since it is a disaster when you catch one of those extra high cards that are still in the deck. The fact is that if you never double-down at all with ace-deuce, you are decreasing your fluctuations and reducing your profits by an insignificant amount.

Bottom Line

Basic Strategy

Hard 13: Hit against seven through ace. Stand against deuce through six.

Soft 13: Double against five through six. Hit against everything else.

If You Are Counting

Hard 13: Hit against a deuce or a trey when the deck gets slightly negative. Hit against four through six when the deck gets moderately negative.

Soft 13: Stop doubling when the deck gets slightly negative.

A Total of 12
(Including Two Aces)

Discussion

is actually quite a bit different from the other "stiffs." Since hitting it will only bust you when you catch a ten, there is about a 9 out of 13 chance that you will survive that hit. Because of that, it is a lot more likely that the correct strategy will be to hit that 12 even against a small card. In fact, the basic strategy play with 12 is to hit it against a deuce or trey, as well, of course, against a seven through ace.

If you are counting it takes only a slightly negative deck for it to be right to hit against anything. (Do not confuse a total of 12 with a dealer's upcard of deuce. Though you would be more apt to hit hands against a deuce than a five, it is still often right to stand against that deuce. It would take a moderately bad deck to make you hit 15 against a deuce showing, but only a slightly bad deck to hit a 12 against a five.) When the deck gets positive you would of course stop hitting 12 as often. Against a slightly positive deck you would stand on 12 against a trey (along with four, five, and six of course), and against a moderately positive deck you would begin to stand on 12 against a deuce. As far as standing with 12 against a high card, that would be a play you would never make unless you had a hidden computer that was counting every card and happened to come up with a weird situation.[17]

As far as a

is concerned, this pair is very similar to the pair of deuces, treys, and sevens. Those pairs you split against four, five, six, and seven when you cannot double after splitting, as well as against deuces and treys when you can. The same is true for sixes, except that you do not split a pair of sixes against specifically a seven. It is easier to memorize the right strategy if you lump pairs of deuces, treys, sixes, and sevens together, but you must remember this exception.

The bottom line is that you split sixes against a four, five, or six if you cannot double down after splitting, and against a deuce, trey, four, five, or six if you can. As far as how to adjust this based on the count, a good approximation to the proper strategy would be that you stop splitting when the deck is moderately negative. Knowing more details than that is of minuscule value.

Now let's get to

---

[17]Hidden computers are illegal in many jurisdictions. So I don't recommend that you carry one.

Common sense tells you that you should split them as much as you can. This is true even though you are only allowed one card on each ace (unlike the other pairs).[18] By doing so you have turned your soft 12 into two 11s. Since you have doubled your bet your net expected value is almost exactly the same as it would be when doubling down on 11. Actually the play is even more advantageous since you not only doubled your bet with 11, but also changed your total. Thus basic strategy says to split two aces against any upcard. And this, for the most part, would not change even if you were counting. It would take a horribly negative deck for you to stop doing it against anything but an ace showing. Even against an ace you split your two aces unless the deck gets moderately negative.

Bottom Line

Basic Strategy

Hard 12: Stand versus four, five, or six. Hit versus deuce, trey, seven, eight, nine, ten, or ace.

Pair of aces: Split versus all upcards.

Pair of sixes: Split versus four through six.

If You Are Counting

Hard 12: Stand against a trey when the deck gets slightly positive. Stand against a deuce when the deck gets moderately positive. Hit against everything including a four, five, or six when the deck gets slightly negative.

---

[18]An exception occurs in a few casinos that allow you to resplit aces if you catch another ace.

Pair of aces: Stop splitting against an ace when the deck is moderately negative.

Pair of sixes: Start splitting versus deuce or trey at slightly positive decks. Stop splitting altogether when the deck is moderately negative.

A Total of 11

Discussion

is, of course, a lovely total. In general, you would rather have it than even a

That statement is partially true because you can double down with it, and it is something you should almost always do when you get it. When you're up against a small card you completely double your expectation by doubling down since you would only take one card regardless (except when you catch an ace and are up against a deuce or a trey). Against a high card the doubling down strategy hurts your chances a little, but your expectation still goes up by doubling since you have bet twice as much.

The single deck basic strategy with 11 is to double down against all upcards. The multiple deck basic strategy makes it a very close decision against an ace. That is, it is almost a coin flip. So if you always double down on 11, including against an ace, the error is almost infinitesimal. In any case, you hopefully have learned to count so that your decisions will be based on the count.

In the case of 11 the only question is whether or not the deck has become negative enough to make you stop doubling down in certain situations. (Obviously once the deck gets positive it is even more advantageous to double down on 11, so you should always do it, even against an ace.)

The rules are:

1.   Stop doubling down against an ace if the deck is at all negative.
2.   Stop doubling down against a ten or nine when the deck is moderately negative.
3.   Stop doubling down against an eight when the deck is highly negative.

It is conceivable that the deck could get so horribly negative that you would be wrong to double down against other upcards as well. But this book does not discuss such situations, and the long run gains from knowing about them are minuscule.

There is one problem with using certain counts to help you to decide whether to double down on an 11. It has to do with the schizophrenic nature of the ace. If you use a count that counts the ace as a high card you will occasionally get bad advice when you have an 11. For instance, if a lot of aces have quickly come out of the deck your count will probably be negative. If you then are dealt an 11 against a nine, you may erroneously refrain from doubling even though those missing aces should make you want to double even more.

The only way to get around this problem is to keep a side count of aces and adjust accordingly. Some professionals do this. However, it is debatable whether or not the extra effort involved helps more than it hurts. Even talented players with excellent memories may be cutting down on their playing time, which costs them more than the small extra gain to their strategy that the side count of aces gives them.

Bottom Line

Basic Strategy

Hard 11: Double down against all upcards.

If You Are Counting

Hard 11: Stop doubling down against an ace if the deck is at all negative. Stop doubling down against a ten or a nine when the deck is moderately negative. Stop doubling down against an eight when the deck is highly negative.

A Total of 10

Discussion

Just as with a total of 11, the only decision is whether to double down or not. Though you do theoretically have the option to split

it can never really be right to do. (There are of course ridiculously extreme situations where it would be right — such as when the dealer is showing a seven, and there is nothing but a bunch of fives remaining in the deck. In that case it would be right to split and wrong to double down, but that situation will never come up and you wouldn't know it if it did.)

The basic strategy play with a

is to double down against everything except a ten or an ace. The play completely doubles your expectation when you are against a four, five, or a six since you would only take one card no matter what you caught anyway. Against a deuce or a trey, it almost completely doubles it since the only time doubling hurts your strategy is when you catch a deuce and would have hit again.

Against a seven through nine, doubling significantly reduces your winning chances, but you are still better off having somewhat lesser chances at double the bet. In the case of the dealer showing a ten or ace however, you normally do better just to hit.

The above strategy changes of course if you are counting. The nice thing about a total of ten is that your count always gives you good advice, even if aces are counted as high cards. The reason, of course, is that when you have a ten you want to catch an ace since it will be counted as 11. And thus it is in the same category as the ten you are counting, not just for betting purposes but in this case for playing purposes as well. Here are the rules as to how you should alter basic strategy with a total of ten as far as the count is concerned:

1. Stop doubling against a nine when the count is slightly negative.
2. Stop doubling against an eight when the deck is moderately negative.
3. Stop doubling against a seven or a deuce if the deck is very negative.
4. *Start* doubling against a ten or an ace when the deck is moderately *positive*.

Most of the above rules are pretty similar to what your common sense ought to tell you. The reason that you can double against a ten or an ace once the deck gets moderately positive has to do with the fact that we already know the dealer does not have a blackjack. You on the other hand still have a decent chance of catching a 21 or at least a 20, while the dealer's chances for 21 are a lot less. Thus the computer tells you to double down to maximize your profit during these moderately positive decks. (It can be frustrating to double down with a total of 10 against a dealer's ten or ace showing, catch bad and have the dealer show you a good hand. In fact, you will occasionally have a streak where you will wish that you didn't listen to this advice. But rest assured that it is correct. When the deck is moderately positive [or better] you earn a little extra money in the long run by making this aggressive play. So just do it.)

Bottom Line

Basic Strategy

Hard 10: Double against everything except a ten or ace.

Pair of fives: Never split.

If You Are Counting

See rules 1 through 4 above.

A Total of 9

Discussion

In 1962 when Thorp first came out with his book *Beat the Dealer*, one of his suggestions that raised some eyebrows was the fact that you should often double down with a

This was considered a sucker play at the time. Common sense tells you that the play seems dubious since your best result would be a total of 20, and a more reasonable optimistic expectation would be 19. Furthermore, doubling down with a nine must decrease your chances of winning no matter what the dealer shows, since you would have always hit it again had you caught a deuce. In spite of these common sense reasons, Thorp and his computer discovered that you do in fact sometimes increase your expected value when you double down on this total. For instance, if the dealer shows a four and you hit your 9, you will win about 57 percent of the time. This is an average win of 14 cents per 1 dollar bet. If you double down, your chances fall to 55 percent, which gains you 10 cents per 1 dollar bet, but since you have bet 2 dollars, it earns you 20 cents.

Using similar reasoning Thorp discovered that the basic strategy for a total of nine was to double down against any upcard, deuce through six. However it was later discovered that it is very close against specifically a deuce, and may not be right in ceratin multiple deck situations. This is similar to the *11 versus ace discussed earlier.* Still it is a fine point that I won't go into detail here. So if you always double down with 9 against deuce through six, any possible error is once again minuscule.

Of course the idea again is to improve on basic strategy based on the count. If you are counting the rules are:

1. Stop doubling down against a deuce, trey, or four if the deck is slightly negative.
2. Stop doubling down against a five or a six if the deck is moderately negative.
3. *Start* doubling down against a seven if the deck is moderately positive.
4. *Start* doubling down against an eight if the deck is very positive.

Again, I think you will find that those rules pretty much follow common sense and thus should be easy to remember. And again, notice that aces are high cards for this decision just as they are in betting decisions, so you need not make any side count adjustments.

Bottom Line

Basic Strategy

Hard 9: Double versus deuce through six.

If You Are Counting

Hard 9: See the four rules above.

A Total of 8

Ace-seven is covered in the chapter on 18.

is a hand that you normally simply hit. That will always be the basic strategy play. However, a counter will sometimes double down with it. It's the right play to make against a six once the deck gets slightly positive. It's right against a five when the deck is moderately positive, and even right against a four once the deck gets highly positive.

As for a

you would never split them if you're playing at a casino that doesn't allow doubling down after splitting. However, at those places that do allow doubling after splitting you should do it (rather than double down on your eight) against a five or a six as long as the deck is not negative, and you should also do it against a four if the deck is slightly positive. Thus, to put it another way, any time you would double down with an eight you are very slightly better off splitting two fours instead, as long as you can double after splitting.

Bottom Line

Basic Strategy

Hard 8: Hit versus all upcards.

Pair of fours: Split versus five or six if you can double after split; otherwise just hit.

If You Are Counting

Hard 8: Double versus six when the deck gets slightly positive. Double versus five when the deck gets moderately positive. Double versus four when the deck gets highly positive.

Pair of fours: Never split if you can't double after splitting. If you can double after splitting you would split against a five or a six unless the deck is slightly negative. You would split against a four only if the deck was at least slightly positive.

A Total of 7

Discussion

We are only going to discuss hard 7 here. A hand like ace-six is a soft 17. So go to the 17 chapter to see how that hand is played. When you have a

the only real decision is whether to double-down or not. The basic strategy play is to hit. However, if the deck is very positive you would double-down against a five or a six, unless you felt like this might bring heat upon you. (If you never make this play, it will have virtually no impact on your long term results since it will so rarely be correct to do, and even when it is correct it gains little.)

Bottom Line

Basic Strategy

Hard 7: Hit versus all upcards.

If You Are Counting

Hard 7: Double versus five or six if the deck gets highly positive.

A Total of 6

Discussion

Ace-five is covered in the chapter on 16.

is obviously a hand that you would always hit. That leaves us with

If you don't split them you have a pretty lousy starting total of 6, and would lose money against any upcard if you simply hit them.

You sometimes do better if you turn these into two hands, both that start off with a trey. It makes a big difference whether you are allowed to double down if you catch a good card when you split. If you can, basic strategy tells you to split your treys all the way from a deuce up to a seven. However if you cannot double down, you only should split your treys against a four through seven. Notice that we are lumping a seven in with the other small cards because of its weakness. However, remember that when you are against a seven you must hit your stiff if either one of your two treys turn into one. As far as the count is concerned it takes a moderately to highly negative deck before you would stop splitting against any of the aforementioned upcards.

Bottom Line

Basic Strategy

Hard 6: Always hit.

Pair of treys: Split versus four through seven.

If You Are Counting

Hard 6: Always hit.

Pair of treys: Stop splitting when the deck gets moderately negative.

A Total of 5

We are not speaking of ace-four. That is "soft 15," and it is covered in the chapter on 15. With a

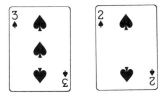

you would simply hit and pray for a six.

A Total of 4

Discussion

Ace-three is soft 14 and is covered in the chapter on 14. The only other 4 is a

a hand you will either hit or split. The basic strategy play is to split against a four, five, six, or seven; otherwise hit. If, however, you can double down after splitting, you should also split against a deuce or a trey. Once again, deuces are very similar to treys, sixes, and sevens as far as when they should be split. And once again, it takes a pretty bad deck for them to be wrong to split against the appropriate (dealer) upcards. But keep in mind that when you do split these deuces against slightly bad decks you'll probably want to hit again if you catch a ten.

Bottom Line

Basic Strategy

Pair of deuces: Split versus four through seven.

If You Are Counting

Pair of deuces: Stop splitting at moderately negative decks.

A Total of 3

You came to the wrong place. The only 3 you can have is

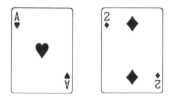

which is soft 13. So go to the 13 chapter.

A Total of 2

A total of 2 means

And two aces is a soft 12, which is where we cover that particular hand. So, just go to 12.

Basic Strategy in a Nutshell

The following is a very close approximation to perfect Basic Strategy.

Hard Hands:
1. Never stand on 11 or less.
2. Never hit on 17 or more.
3. Hit 12 through 16 versus a seven through ace.
4. Hit 12 versus a deuce or trey.
5. Stand on 12 through 16 deuce through six. (Exception: Hit 12 versus a deuce or trey as per Number 4.)
6. Double with 11 versus all upcards.
7. Double with 10 versus a deuce through nine.
8. Double with 9 versus a deuce through six.

Soft Hands:
1. Never stand on 17 or less.
2. Never hit on 19 or more.
3. Hit 18 versus a nine, ten, or ace.
4. If you can double down on soft 18 you should do it against a trey, four, five, and six, and merely stand against a deuce, seven, and eight. If you can't double you should stand against all of these upcards deuce through eight.
5. Double on soft 13 through soft 17 versus a four, five, or six; hit otherwise. (This rule is very slightly inaccurate.)

Pairs:
1. Always split aces and eights.
2. Never split tens, fives, or fours.
3. Split nines versus all but seven, ten, or ace.
4. Split deuces, treys, sixes, and sevens, against four through seven. (Add treys if you can double after splitting.) Exception: Don't split sixes against a seven.

Strategy Changes
in a Nutshell

The following is a summary of all the important strategy deviations (and most of the not so important ones) that you will make from basic strategy according to the count. And by that, of course, I mean the true count (running count divided by the number of decks remaining).

A. When the deck is at least slightly positive you start:
1.   Standing on 16 against a ten (if you can't surrender).
2.   Standing on 12 against a trey.
3.   Doubling on 8 against a six.
4.   Doubling on soft 19 against a five or a six.

B. When the deck is at least moderately positive you start:
1.   Buying insurance.
2.   Standing on 16 against an ace (if you can't surrender).
3.   Standing on 15 against a ten (if you can't surrender).
4.   Standing on 12 against a deuce.
5.   Doubling down on 10 against a ten or an ace.
6.   Doubling down on 9 against a seven.
7.   Doubling down on 8 against a five.
8.   Doubling down on soft 19 against a four.
9.   Splitting nines against a seven or an ace.

C. When the deck gets highly positive you start:
1.   Standing on 16 against a nine (if you can't surrender).
2.   Standing on 15 against an ace (if you can't surrender).
3.   Doubling down on 8 against a four.
4.   Doubling down on soft 19 against a four.
5.   Doubling down on soft 20 against a five or a six.
6.   Splitting two nines against a seven.
7.   Splitting two tens against a five or a six.

D. When the deck is at least slightly negative you start:
1. Hitting all 12s.
2. Hitting 13 against a deuce or a trey.
3. Refraining from doubling down with 11 against an ace.
4. Refraining from doubling down with a 10 against a nine.
5. Refraining from doubling down with a 9 against a deuce, trey, or four.
6. Refraining from doubling down with soft 13 and 14 against everything.
7. Refraining from splitting two eights against an ace (but only in games where the dealer hits soft 17).

E. When the deck is at least moderately negative you start:
1. Hitting 13 against a four and a five.
2. Hitting 14 against a deuce.
3. Refraining from doubling down with 11 against a nine or a ten.
4. Refraining from doubling down with 10 against an eight.
5. Refraining from doubling down with 9 against everything.
6. Refraining from splitting aces against an ace.
7. Refraining from splitting nines against a deuce, trey, and four.

F. When the deck gets highly negative you start:
1. Hitting all 13s.
2. Hitting 14 against a trey or a four.
3. Hitting 15 against a deuce.
4. Refraining form all doubling down.
5. Refraining from splitting nines against all upcards.

The above information is at least 99 percent accurate. I simplified just a tiny bit in a couple of cases to avoid needless complexity. I doubt if that simplification will cost you even one bet a month in expected value. It ought not to be that hard to learn everything on this list. The reason is that most of the rules follow an obvious pattern and are more or less common sense, especially once you have read and understood everything up to this point. If not, a second reading ought to do the trick.

Part Three

In the Casino

In the Casino

Introduction

Just because you now know how to play blackjack with an edge, doesn't mean that it is a simple matter to turn that knowledge into lots of money. Besides knowing how to play well, there are a few more things you must do. They are:

1. Find good games.
2. Disguise your expertise so that those games will stay good.
3. Do not overbet your bankroll.
4. Play your best at all times.

We will discuss the first three ideas shortly. As for Number 4, realize that there is a difference between *knowing* how to play good blackjack and actually doing it in the casino. You cannot let yourself be distracted by the environment or worry about any individual hand if it will cause you to lose count or play incorrectly. This is more difficult for some than others, but anybody can do it with practice. There is not much more to say about that.

As far as the other three points are concerned, I will give you a brief overview of the relevant ideas. Many of the blackjack books listed in the recommended readings will go into greater detail. You really should read them if you are planning to become a very serious blackjack player. However, most of what you need to know will be discussed in this section.

What Makes a Good Game?

If you are a counter you will have an edge over almost any blackjack game. However, that edge can vary significantly depending on how good a game you are up against. The best games can give you an advantage of 1 percent or more. Lousy games are frequently worth less than a half a percent. The following factors determine how good a game is:
1. The number of decks.
2. The house rules.
3. The degree of penetration.
4. The number of hands per hour.
5. The tolerance of bet spreads.
6. The heat on big bets.

Let's look at these factors one at a time.

Factor No. 1: Number of decks. Theoretically you are better off playing against a single deck. You start off with a smaller disadvantage and you don't have to spread your bets as much to put the odds in your favor. On the other hand, there is much more heat on a single deck game. Shoe games are much more likely to allow a much bigger betting spread. This subject will be discussed in greater detail in the next chapter.

Factor No. 2: House rules. Not all casinos play by the same rules. Some house rules help the player quite a bit more than others. Everything else being equal, the main things a serious blackjack player should look for are:
1. The dealer standing on soft seventeen.
2. The option to double down on any two cards.
3. The option to double down after splitting a pair.
4. The option to surrender.

There are other variations in rules as well, but those are the main ones. If you can find a casino that gives you the best of all of these rules you should probably play there. In fact, if these rules are coupled with a single deck game, basic strategy itself will give you a tiny edge! However it is unlikely you will find a single deck game with all of these attributes.

Factor No. 3: Degree of Penetration. Keep in mind that I said you choose the best rules *if everything else is equal.* But that is often not the case. The biggest single factor that can make up for a discrepancy in rules between two casinos is their degree of penetration. By that I mean how far down they deal before shuffling. If you are an expert counter this factor is tremendously important, especially if the casino tolerates a large bet spread. For instance, a casino that deals 75 percent of a single deck with bad rules is worth more money to you than one that deals 40 percent of a single deck with good rules. Against a six deck shoe, a casino that deals four of those six decks is not nearly as good as one that deals five of those six decks before shuffling. This particular subject is treated in much greater detail by Arnold Snyder. I would recommend his books to all serious players, if only for that reason.

Factor No. 4: Number of hands per hour. What determines how many hands you get per hour is mainly the number of other players at the table. At a full table you will only get about 60 hands per hour if you are playing only one spot. If you are playing head up you could be dealt as many as 250 hands per hour. Clearly, more hands per hour ought to add to your hourly rate of win. This is especially true if you are playing against a single deck. Single deck pros typically do not bet that much money, since the heat is too intense if they do. But even a $25 single deck bettor can make close to $100 per hour if he is playing head ups and knows what he is doing. On the other hand, if he tries to bet more than a maximum of about $50, the already high heat he will get at a single deck game will tend to get even worse if he is playing heads up.

In the case of multiple decks, a crowded table is not that bad. The reason is that the vast majority of hands do not give you an edge. Therefore, the fact that other players are playing hands doesn't hurt you most of the time. In fact, if when the deck gets good you not only increase your bet, but also bet more than one hand at a time, the crowded table doesn't really hurt you at all. (Another advantage of a crowded table will sometimes be that there is a player betting a lot more than you at that table. Thus he will figure to be getting the most scrutiny.)

Factor No. 5: Tolerance of bet spreads. Again, Arnold Snyder and others discuss this concept in detail. The general idea is that you want to bet as little as possible with a disadvantage and as much as possible with an advantage. This, however, is much more important when you are playing against a multiple deck. Against a single deck there is little extra to be gained spreading your bets higher than a 4-to-1 ratio. But against multiple decks, where you so often are playing with the worst of it, you would like to be able to move your bets at a 20-to-1 ratio, or more. The bottom line is that if one casino tolerates, let's say twice as big a bet spread as another casino, that could make up for worse rules or worse penetration. (When I say tolerate, I mean they will not start shuffling on you, or worse yet, bar you, if you try to spread your bets more than they like.)

Factor No. 6: Heat on big bets. This, of course, does not apply unless you have decided to become a high roller. But if you have, you should know that some casinos are more likely to make their game less good against big money. This usually simply means that they will shuffle sooner. Thus it is possible that when choosing between two casinos, you might choose one that was in the past a bit worse, because it doesn't change its policies when it sees black chips. Almost certainly bigger bets will result in a smaller percentage advantage to you. But if you can keep this syndrome to a minimum you will still make more money in the long run.

How Many Decks
Should You Play Against?

Now that you have hopefully become an expert blackjack player, the next step is to figure out the best way of extracting money from casinos using your expertise. One of the first decisions you will have to make is whether to go after single deck games or shoe games. There are advantages and disadvantages to both approaches. One great advantage to single decks is that mere basic strategy gives you very very close to an even game. Depending on the rules, the house edge against a basic strategy player is usually somewhere between 0.3 percent and nothing at all. A second advantage to single decks is that moderately high, positive true counts occur often.

Contrast this with a six deck shoe. Here, basic strategy yields from about 0.3 percent to over 0.5 percent house advantage, depending on the rules, and the deck gets good only a fairly small percentage of the time. The net result of these differences is that you can beat a single deck with a much smaller bet spread than what would be required for a shoe.

Against a single deck you can have a decent advantage betting one chip against bad decks and two chips against good decks, especially if you are using your count to play better than pure basic strategy. In fact, good players have a small edge over a single deck even when flat betting the same amount every hand! (As long as the dealer deals out somewhere around half the deck. In the case of a six deck shoe you must spread your bets in at least a 10-to-1 ratio from your big bets to your smallest, so that your big bets with an advantage will more than overcome your many smaller bets with a disadvantage.)

From the foregoing arguments it would seem like your decision is an easy one; play against a single deck. Unfortunately it is not so simple, especially if you are betting serious money.

The reason is *heat*. It is now so widely known that single decks are easy to beat that those casinos that offer them are very vigilant against possible winning players. If they don't bar them, they will certainly shuffle up on them. One way to counteract this is by trying to disguise even your small bet spread. For instance, you can make your big bet right off the top and only reduce when the deck is bad *and you have lost your previous hand.* Never bet more than your bet off the top.

Many casinos will fall for this, and you still have a significant edge. This will almost certainly work if your big bet is one $25 chip and your small bet is one $5 chip. It might even work if your big bet is a black $100 chip and your small bet is a green $25 chip.

Certainly if you are betting small amounts you should play only against a single deck. You are unlikely to be stopped and your edge is greater. However, once your bets reach any significant size it is unlikely that any camouflage will allow you to play very long in an expert fashion against a single deck. That is why so many pros do in fact play against the shoes. Most casinos still do not realize that their shoes are vulnerable. Thus you can most likely spread, for instance, from $25 all the way up to $500. Of course, this requires a bankroll in the neighborhood of $50,000, while you are trying to win an average of not much more than $100 an hour.

Playing a single deck, betting an average of $25 requires a bankroll in the $5,000 range, and your profits, especially if you play mainly heads up, could be close to $50 an hour. Personally, I think that single decks can still be exploited for a nice weekly wage by expert players who don't have that big a bankroll or who want to avoid the large fluctuations. On the other hand, if you are attempting to make very big money, most casinos have at least a $1,000 limit, you now have no choice but to play shoes. If you are playing shoes, one thing you can do to reduce your fluctuations is to start a team of players that pools their money, as was mentioned earlier. Again, however, this has its own problems.

There is a compromise between one deck games and shoe games. That is, the two deck games. However, the initial disadvantage against two decks is almost as high as it is against four or six decks. Yet the heat on two decks can get almost as high as on one. Everything being equal, two decks is preferable to four. Mainly because two deck games reach decent counts a lot more often. So if you can find a two deck game that allows a high bet spread, you would prefer it over a shoe. This however has not been my experience. Unless things have changed recently your best alternatives are almost certainly the one deck game or the multi-deck game.

Betting Strategy

Most professional blackjack players win mainly because of the way they vary their bets. Expert counters vary their strategy as well, but it is the bet variation that accounts for the largest portion of their edge. (The only possible exception are single deck games, which I will explain shortly.)

When playing against a multi-deck shoe it is critical that your biggest bets be quite a bit larger than your average bets. The reason is that advantageous situations do not come up that often, so most of your hands are played with a disadvantage. Only about 10 percent of the hands that you play will be against a decently high true count shoe.[19] And these are the hands where you make your money. Furthermore, the money you make in these spots has to overcome the money you have lost the other 90 percent of the time when you do not have an advantage. So clearly, your big bets with an advantage must be a lot greater than the bets you make with a disadvantage. (There is a technique that some pros use called "backcounting." The idea is to count the deck while you are a spectator, and only jump in once the shoe gets good. However, there are many casinos that will not let you do this. Even those that will let you quickly catch on to what you are doing, so I don't recommend the technique.)

To beat a shoe, your big bets need to be at least ten times as big as your small bets. The problem is that large bet spreads bring on scrutiny from the pit. Even those floor men who know little about blackjack, do know that the large bet spreads are the hallmark of the professional player. Then again, many non-pros also spread their bets quite a bit. Furthermore, it is still not widely known that shoes are targeted by counters, which means that if

---

[19]10 percent is a very rough estimate. The actual percentage depends on the number of decks, the house rules, and most importantly, how far down they deal.

you are careful you ought to be able to get away with that 10-to-1 or greater spread.

One thing that you should almost never do is jump directly from your smallest bet to your largest, regardless of how good the count has become. That would definitely "wake up" a lot of pit bosses. Generally your bet should never be more than twice the previous bet. This means it would take a few hands to work up to your maximum. There are a few other tricks you can use as well.

Suppose you sit at a table, planning to bet anywhere from $25 to $500 per hand. The best strategy is to buy-in only about $200. Since you are starting off at the beginning of the shoe, you know that your first several bets will almost certainly be one green chip. If, on the other hand, you had made a much bigger buy-in and still started betting this small, you would be immediately tipping off the pit that you may well be betting much bigger later. So they will worry about you right from the git-go. When you buy-in $200, no one thinks anything of it. Often you will never bet much more than that minimum bet, so the pit will never even consider the possibility that you were counting.

Another important tip would be to start moving up your bet (at a very small positive [true] count) *before* the deck becomes advantageous. Any pit boss who is counting along with you is apt to think that you are not a winning player, since you will be making moderate bets with no edge or even a slight disadvantage. But by betting this way you have put yourself in a position to quickly get to your top bet, if in fact the deck gets good shortly thereafter. When the deck does get good, your previous bet was in the $100 range. If you won it, it should be a natural progression to go to $200, and if you lost, you can feign disgust and pull out more money, and now change color and become a larger bettor.

There are other tricks as well. The general idea being to find ways to spread your bets quite a bit without giving away your expertise. Different strategies are probably needed for different casinos.

If you are playing against a single deck you do not need to spread your bets as much. There is no way that you could, since casinos are much more paranoid when it comes to single decks. Luckily, however, you don't need to spread that much to have an edge. This is mainly because you will be playing at least one out of three hands with an advantage. Furthermore, most of the other hands that you play will be bucking only a slight disadvantage. This is especially true because strategy variations are more important against a single deck, and come up more often than against a shoe.

If the single deck that you are playing against has good rules, betting one or two units is all you need to do to have a nice edge (as long as they deal at least half of the deck). Beware, however, of games that only allow you to double down on 10 or 11. Against them you would really be a lot happier if you could bet a 3-to-1 spread.

If you want to be even more cautious about heat against a single deck, you can temper your spread even more by betting two units right off the top, and never increasing your bet unless you won the previous hand. This hurts you a little bit mathematically, since that first bet has a slight disadvantage, plus you are often betting only one unit when you do have an advantage. (This would happen anytime you lost your previous one unit bet.)

When I was playing seriously I used the following method against a single deck: I would buy in $500, and ask for $200 in green ($25) chips and $300 in black ($100) chips. Then I would use a similar technique to the one described above, except in this case I would never *decrease* my bet after a win. I always either bet one black chip or one green chip, and I always started the deck with a black chip. Any time I won a black chip bet, I'd bet it again. This means I would often make many consecutive maximum bets against negative decks. Of course if I did, it meant that I won every one of them, except maybe the last. If I lost a black chip bet, what I bet next depended on the count. If it was bad, I'd cut back to one green chip. After I bet a green chip, what I bet next would again depend on the count. So you can see that this method occasionally goes against the count. I'd make a max bet off the top, without an edge, and I'd make a max bet whenever the previous hand was a max bet winner. Sometimes this was against a bad deck. However, in spite of these occasional suboptimal bets, I still had a big edge. Keep in mind that good counters should be able to at least break even flat-betting against a single deck, if they know how to change their strategy. And of course, my method is a lot better than that. I would always make a max bet whenever the deck was good, and I would usually be making a small bet when the deck was bad.

In fact, this method might very well be superior to religiously betting one or two units at the proper times. (I would like to see someone simulate a comparison on a computer.) For although I would sometimes be making the "wrong" bet, I was also employing a 4-to-1 spread. (Keep in mind the reason this strategy works well is because it involves one chip, which I can carelessly flick out, apparently on a whim. If, for instance, I tried to make my small bet $50 and my big bet $200, this would undoubtedly seem much less natural and cause greater consternation in the pit.)

The idea is to try to combine what you know is the mathematically proper betting variation, with the real life factors that you will be facing as a serious blackjack player. This means that you've got to give up a little bit mathematically to increase the chances that you'll get the game you want. Your betting strategy is one way to help accomplish this goal. There are other ways as well, which we will come to shortly.

Quitting a Negative Shoe

Here's a trick that should add a little bit to your profits. When playing against six or eight decks it is important to understand that the true count will not change quickly and that the casino's initial advantage is higher than in a hand held game. Thus, it is important to quit the game if the count goes negative. This usually means -4 or -5 early in the shoe, and as little as -2 after three or more decks are in play.

For instance, suppose against a six deck shoe you are dealt on the very first hand

against the dealer's

If it doesn't look too obvious, change tables.

The drain on your bankroll from playing against negative decks won't be as great, and in the same amount of time you will be able to find more favorable situations.

Dealing with Casino Heat

As we have seen, playing blackjack is a bit of a cat and mouse game. The casino is the cat, and blackjack is the means to the cheese. Thus the house will carefully watch its players to determine if there is a skilled counter present. Generally they are not that good at this, but they do try, and almost all casinos are known to bar players.

Two pieces of advice that should help you are:
1.   Don't overplay your casino.
2.   Don't verbalize.

The first piece of advice actually comes in two parts. Don't play too long at any one time — in most casinos 45 minutes to an hour should be the max — and don't play too many days in succession on the same shift.

You should use your judgment. But at most major casinos after playing three or four days in a week requires a subsequent break of a couple of months. In addition, if you have a big win, give it a rest even if you had planned on playing longer.

The blackjack literature is filled with players using a successful act to fool the blackjack pit personnel. There is the crazy man and the drunk, both achieving huge betting spreads and making a "big score." My experience is that it doesn't work this way. If they don't know or remember you, you will be welcome to play again. Keep your head down, don't say much, and don't give them a reason to recognize you the next time you show up.

If you do get barred it is best to politely pick up your chips and leave. If possible cash them in another day. Don't hassle with the pit; their decision is already made, and it is always final. Now give that casino at least a six month rest and don't play on that shift for at least a year. You will be able to return again.

Being barred is not the end of the world. It is something that happens to all good blackjack players, but something that you wish to minimize. If you follow this advice you should not be asked to leave too often. Those players who find themselves barred in "every casino in Las Vegas," are not as expert as they think they are.

Team Play

Suppose you had a $1,000 bankroll and found a game with a 1 percent edge. If you bet all $1,000 dollars on one hand you would "earn" $10. That is your mathematical expectation. The problem is that in real life that bet wouldn't really make you $10. Rather it would either make you $1,000 or cost you $1,000. The bad part is that you will go broke and be out of action almost 50 percent of the time. But let's say you were allowed instead to simultaneously make 1,000 $1 bets. In this case you would still earn $10. The difference is there would be no chance of going broke. In fact, it is very unlikely you wouldn't be ahead. The general point to be made here is that if you split a big bet into simultaneous smaller bets you make just as much with a far smaller chance of blowing all of your money. On the other hand, you can make your separate bets total more than a single bet, still have a smaller chance of going broke, yet increase your expectation.

The problem with the above scenario is that there is no way you can, as an individual, make simultaneous bets. (You could, of course, take more than one hand. The problem is that the bets are not independent. Because the dealer may have a very good hand, multiple bets at one table do not cut down on volatility as much as multiple bets at different tables would. You also could make your smaller bets not simultaneous, but that takes more time and reduces your hourly win rate.)

Blackjack players, however, discovered a way to get around this problem. What they did was form teams. As an example, let's say five expert blackjack players each had a $20,000 bankroll. This means that each of their maximum bets, when playing individually, should be about $100. Their hourly win rate would be about $50 an hour each. If instead those five players pooled their money, and all played out of the same bankroll, they would have a team with $100,000 available to them, and each player could bet as high as $500 while they were playing simultaneously at different tables. The whole team thus figures to earn $1,250 an hour or $250 per hour per player.[20] At least that is the theory. I personally have never been a member of a blackjack team. However, I know that things don't always run as smoothly as theory would indicate. Obviously the first problem is the honesty of all of the players. There are many other logistical problems as well. Again, for a more detailed overview of team play I would recommend some of the other books mentioned in "Appendix C."

---

[20] I use these figures just to illustrate the mathematics. In real life you would encounter tougher games if you were betting $500 a hand, thus cutting into your hourly win rate.

A Note on Comps

Casinos are known to have great comps. There are the gourmet meals, the fabulous shows, and the great rooms. I know from experience that comps add a lot to the casino and blackjack experience. But my advice is not to push for them. This is because to earn comps requires that you be "rated," and being rated means additional scrutiny. That means that your days as a successful blackjack player in that casino can be numbered.

On the other hand, if you are betting big money it appears unnatural not to be rated, and if you are offered a comp you should of course take it. (This will frequently happen if you are a new customer in the casino.) However, if you do enjoy a gourmet meal or a show, keep in mind that the casino host may show up to say hello and see how you are doing. So if you don't use your real name make sure that everyone in your party knows what adjustment to make.

Here is some other advice on being rated:

1. You don't have to give your real name. Many people who get rated don't use their real names, so you don't have to feel uncomfortable doing this.

2. Don't tell the pit where you are staying. They can always call that casino if they become suspicious of your play to verify if you are a "real" customer. One associate of mine always told the pit that he was "staying with my sister" who lived in town. He never had any problems.

3. Always use the same name on the same shift. Communication between shifts is very poor in some casinos, but you must be aware that it is the pit's job to remember their customers. Even though you hope that they will forget you, if they remember you with a different name, they will become suspicious.

4. If you are going to ask for a comp, the best time is just after a big loss. Of course, you may not feel as hungry or be in the

mood to be entertained. However, pit personnel will frequently be sympathetic to your plight. A friend of mine once asked for a comp after a big loss when playing only one shoe in a major Las Vegas casino. The pit boss told him that since he didn't play very long he needed a reason to give him a comp. "I can give you 5,800 reasons," my friend replied. Needless to say, he got his comp.

Conclusion

If you follow everything in this book you will win playing "21." It's that simple. You will have a mathematical edge over the house that must make you money (in the long run). You can even use this book to become a professional blackjack player. And you need no other book. Good as they are, those other more complex manuals will add little to your profits (though I do recommend that you read a few of them if you turn pro).

Keep in mind, however, that your edge over the house will be in the overall neighborhood of about one half of one percent. That means less than a bet an hour. And it means you will have many losing streaks and need an adequate bankroll to sustain them. Also remember that knowing proper strategy is only part (a large part) of beating the game. Finding the best games and keeping "heat" off you are the other parts. Without doing everything right you won't win as much as you could. But even if you don't do everything right, you will definitely have an edge merely from following proper strategy. An edge that figures to make you money whether you happen to be a professional gambler or a weekend player.

So read this book one more time and then get to work.

The following two appendixes on "The Game of Blackjack" and "Playing at the Table" are excerpts from the Fundamentals of "21" *by Mason Malmuth and Lynne Loomis.*

Appendix A

The Game of Blackjack

The object of blackjack is to make a total higher than the dealer's total without going over 21. If your total exceeds 21 — that is, if you bust — you lose even if the dealer also goes over 21. This is the casino's main advantage. Since you must act first, you can lose regardless of what the dealer does.

But you also have some advantages. In most casinos, you have the options of splitting pairs and of doubling down on certain hands. These options allow you to put more money on the table in favorable situations and, when used properly, can be very advantageous. In addition, when you are dealt a blackjack — an ace and a 10-value card — you will get paid three units for every two units that you've bet.

A typical casino blackjack game is played using anywhere from one deck to eight decks of cards. (Games using three decks, five decks, and seven decks of cards are seldom, if ever, seen, although there is no reason why an odd number of decks could not be used.) Single- and double-deck games are generally dealt by hand, whereas games using a larger number of decks are dealt from a wooden box called a "shoe."

All cards are assigned their rank values, with the exception of face cards and aces. Face cards carry a value of 10, and an ace — at the player's option — is worth either 1 or 11 (although an ace cannot be counted as 11 if it puts a player over 21).

As already noted, if the first two cards dealt to you are an ace and either a ten or a face card, you have a blackjack — also known as a "natural" — and will receive a 3-to-2 payoff. If the dealer has a blackjack and you don't, you will lose your original bet. If both you and the dealer have a blackjack, a tie is declared and no money changes hands.

Should you be dealt two cards of the same rank, you have the option to split your pair. That is, you may separate your cards into two hands and put up an additional amount of money equal to your original bet. You will receive cards on both hands, which you now play against the dealer. Most casinos will allow you to split again if you catch another card of the same rank. The exception is aces, which in most houses can be split only once. In addition, when you split a pair of aces, you will receive only one additional card on each hand.

If you do not have the option of splitting, you may be permitted to double down — post an additional amount of money equal to your original bet — on certain hands. When you exercise this option, you will receive only one more card. Most casinos in Las Vegas allow doubling down on any first two cards, but some houses restrict this option to only those hands in which the first two cards total either 10 or 11.

If you don't split or double down, you will have the option to hit or to stand. That is, either you may ask for additional cards — as long as your total is not over 21 — or you may declare that you do not want any more cards. When you are satisfied with your hand — assuming, of course, that you don't bust — the dealer will play out his hand, then will compare his total to your total. You win if the dealer busts or if your total is closer to 21 than his; the dealer wins if you bust or if his total is closer to 21 than yours. If both you and the dealer have the same total, no money changes hands. This is known as a "push."

Appendix B
Playing at the Table

The game of "21" is played at a semicircular table that seats six or seven players. Also present will be the house dealer. After making your buy-in and placing the number of chips you wish to wager in your betting space, you will receive your first two cards.

Depending on the game, your first two cards will be dealt either face up or face down. Single- and double-deck games are generally dealt face down, while in most shoe games, the cards are distributed face up.

In a face-down game, you are permitted to lift your cards slightly above the table surface in order to see them and determine their total. If you are satisfied with your hand — that is, you wish to stand pat — slide your cards face down beneath your chips in the betting space.

STAND PAT

If you want another card, when it is your turn to act, pick up your two cards and scrape them toward you on the felt in one or two quick motions. This will indicate to the dealer that you want a "hit," and he will then give you a card face up on the table.

After receiving one or more cards in this manner, when you are satisfied with your total, slide your two downcards under your chips in the betting space. If you have gone over a total of 21, turn your cards face up and place them in front of your betting space. The dealer will then collect your cards, along with your wager.

If you are permitted to double down and wish to exercise this option, turn both of your cards face up and place an additional wager of equal value next to your original wager. The dealer will then give you one more card, which is dealt face down.

DOUBLING DOWN

Should you wish to split a pair, turn both of your cards face up, separate them, and place an additional bet of equal value next to your original bet.

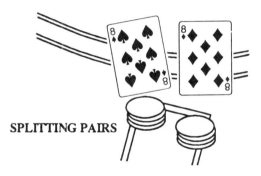

SPLITTING PAIRS

You now will have two hands and will play the one on your right to completion first. Blackjack etiquette dictates that you should not touch your cards after splitting. Consequently, to indicate that you want a "hit," scrape your hand or one of your fingers toward you on the felt. The dealer will then give you a card face up on the table. If you wish to stand pat, hold your hand palm down above your cards and wave it sideways. Once you are satisfied with your first hand, you will then play your second hand to completion in the same manner.

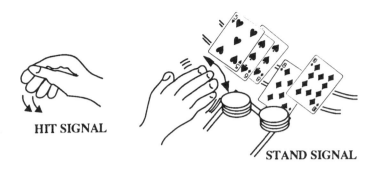

HIT SIGNAL

STAND SIGNAL

As mentioned earlier, when you split a pair of aces, the dealer will give you only one additional card, which is dealt face down, on each hand. Therefore, no signals are necessary.

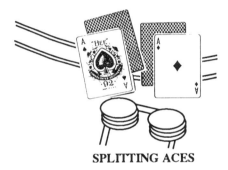

SPLITTING ACES

In a blackjack game that is dealt face up, you should never touch your cards. The hand signals just described should be used to indicate whether you wish to hit or stand. When splitting or doubling down, place an additional bet in front of you on the table and verbally inform the dealer of what you wish to do.

It also should be noted here that as a courtesy to the dealer — and to protect yourself — you should not retrieve your winnings or place your next wager until the dealer has discarded all of your cards.

Finally, if you are not sure of the correct procedure, ask the dealer. It is his job not only to deal the cards and to collect and pay bets, but also to ensure that the game runs smoothly. Most dealers will be glad to give you any assistance you require.

Appendix C
Recommended Reading

1. *Basic Blackjack* by Stanford Wong (1995: Pi Yee Press).

2. *Beat the Dealer* by Edward O. Thorp (1966: Vintage Books).

3. *Beat the One- (Two-, Four-, Six-, Eight-) Deck Game* by Arnold Snyder (1987: RGE Publishing).

4. *Blackbelt in Blackjack* by Arnold Snyder (1998 : RGE Publishing).

5. *Blackjack Essays* by Mason Malmuth (1996: Two Plus Two Publishing).

6. *Blackjack Forum* by Arnold Snyder (Quarterly: RGE Publishing).

7. *Blackjack Secrets* by Stanford Wong (1993: Pi Yee Press).

8. *Blackjack Wisdom* by Arnold Snyder (1997: RGE Publishing)

9. *Current Blackjack News* by Stanford Wong (Monthly: Pi Yee Press).

10. *Fundamentals of Blackjack* by Carlson R. Chambliss and Thomas C. Roginski (1990: Gambler's Book Club Press).

11. *Fundamentals of "21"* by Mason Malmuth and Lynne Loomis (1995: Two Plus Two Publishing).

12. *Gambling for a Living* by David Sklansky and Mason Malmuth (1998: Two Plus Two Publishing)

13. *Million Dollar Blackjack* by Ken Uston (1995: Carol Publishing Group).

14. *Professional Blackjack* by Stanford Wong (1994: Pi Yee Press).

15. *Read the Dealer* by Steve Forte (1986: RGE Publishing).

16. *The Theory of Blackjack* by Peter Griffin (1996: Huntington Press).

17. *Turning the Tables on Las Vegas* by Ian Andersen (1978: Vintage Books).

Index